HEBE'S

Hebe Francis Thyra Fricker in 1929

Hebe with Teazle, Great Dane Griselda and James in 1940

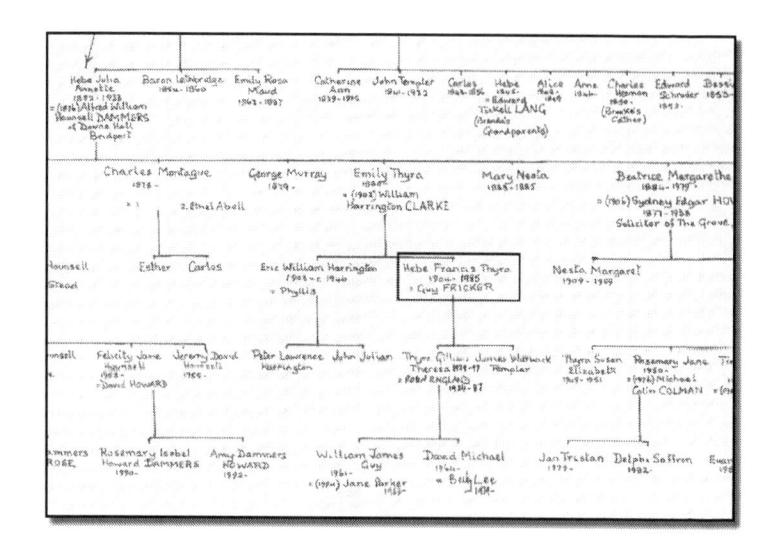

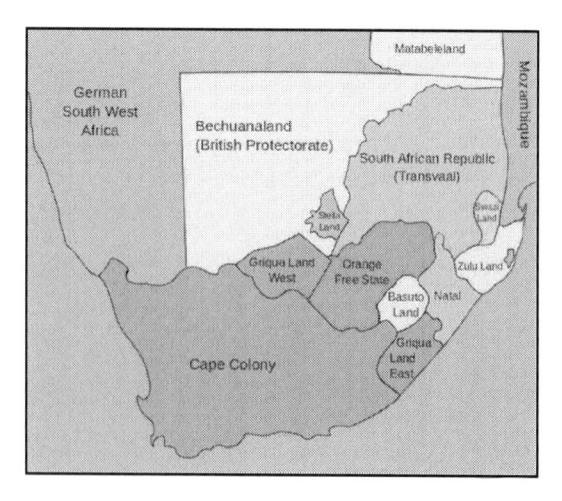

Dedication

This book has been compiled from Hebe's hand-typed manuscript to be enjoyed by each of her 6 great-grandchildren, George, Eliza, Isaac, Ben, Guy, and Lydia.

ARGONAUTS IN EAST GRIQUALAND

FOREWORD

In writing my recollections of life on a South African farm, from 1937–1946, naturally things come back to me as they were then. Now, forty years on, conditions must have altered drastically, e.g. tractors on every farm, replacing the patient ox.

I realise it is no longer customary to refer to the Africans as natives or boys; I understand they prefer "Blacks". I have written as I remembered, and hope no-one would think the terms we used then, were ever thought derogatory in any way. I have always had the greatest respect and regard for the Africans, as I hope will be obvious in my writings.

Although horses have come into so much of my life, I do realise that there must be some of my readers who have no particular interests in that direction. For them, may I suggest some mild skimming, e.g. chapters 3, 5, 6, 7, 16 and 28 may well be omitted, and some tedium relieved.

CHAPTER 1

Arrival in South Africa. First impressions

South Africa and the first sight of that imposing view of Table Mountain – all rather an anti-climax perhaps, certainly for the seven-year-old[1] who had said, "When we get to South Africa, will Fa be standing on the edge?" We still had another few days ahead of us in the ship, round the coast to Durban.

The voyage had not felt much like the idle, sun-bathing, luxurious laze so often advertised. Two children of seven and three made sure there were enough chores to save me from boredom at least.

We were glad to get our shore legs for a day or two, and the children played on the sand. I found the old Dutch architecture among the wine estates, Mediterranean type coast scenery, and the dominating background of Table Mountain in all its aspects, together fulfilled the claims made everywhere for the beauty of the peninsula. But the Cape has its own very definite individuality and was no guide to the part of the country where we were bound, up-country East Griqualand.

I had no real conception of what I should expect. Towns where we put in, as the ship came round the coast, only repelled. Alien, dusty, glaring places, which seemed to have no beauty in those first nostalgic days. There was an atmosphere of squalor in the back streets, so utterly different from that of the London slums, yet as familiar in its depression.

There was an almost tangible felling of distrust, I had not yet discovered the true quality of the African, and it was not in the towns that I was to get release. Indeed, I felt a prisoner those first days, the

---

[1] Teazle – William and Michael England's mother

shackles were heavy, and their weight increased with the heat and the unaccustomed sounds and smells. The palms and tropical vegetation looked tawdry and forbidding in turn. The bright colouring of white houses, red roofs, gay flowers, seemed only glib, too gay, lacking depth and therefore unsatisfying, even mocking; inimical, if I allowed them through my defences.

Inland from the coast, the country was unsatisfactory, a hundred senseless bushes marred the clean lines of the hills, dotted about everywhere they were merely an unsightly rash on the face of a landscape that might otherwise have promised to be fair. This first impression of the coast has not altered, but now I have the knowledge of the utter satisfaction to be found up-country.

My husband had been a Regular Officer, but tiring of peacetime soldiering, decided to retire from the Army as a Captain. He toyed with the ideas of many different jobs, Chief Constable, and Russian Interpreter among them. The latter would have involved a fairly lengthy stay in Russia to learn the language thoroughly; with a young family (our youngest child only just over a year old) there would have been problems. Then at a Guest Night in the Regiment, he met a retired Colonel, who had gone to South Africa to live for his health. He had suspect lungs and the climate and altitude of East Griqualand proved to be ideal. He bought a farm, which gave him a great interest, although he depended on a nephew, born in the country, and having a farming background, to manage the farm for him. Colonel P.B. told my husband all about it, and with the possible influence of a good Guest night, he decided to follow that lead and consider farming himself. He went to the village blacksmith after handing in his papers, and got some valuable instruction on the repair of farm implements. The local carpenter gave him useful tips on working with wood, and he picked up what he could in D.I.Y. lines, as it would be termed today. The Colonel had warned him there would be no "little men" around the corner to be called in. Self-reliance would be essential, although neighbouring farmers proved to be unfailing in their readiness to give advice and help in emergencies.

Thanks to Colonel P.B. who arranged it, a farmer in East Griqualand offered to take Guy on his farm, and give him most necessary experience, not only in farming, but also in dealings with the African labour. Thus he went out to South Africa, a country which appealed to him especially, as he had been born in the Cape; although he came back to Europe with his wonderful Mother[2], and his brothers and sisters, at an early age.

Meanwhile, I was parked with the two children for two years, partly staying with Guy's Mother, partly with my own parents. Both families most generously bearing the burden, and making the whole project possible.

After that two years, the same Colonel P.B. and his most charming and delightful wife (an artist) invited me to bring the children and stay on their farm, while they took a long leave in England. Guy could assist the nephew on the farm, we could "learn" the country. So we arrived, and after a night in Durban, set off for East Griqualand in an ancient Buick, just purchased in time by my husband for eighty pounds.

It nobly transported us and our immediate needs up from the coast to the 5,000 ft. of our destination. From Pietermaritzburg onwards the roads were dust and pot-holes (or deep mud in the rains of summer). Eventually a small voice from the back, where James, aged three, was perched on some of our bundles, uttered the now much-quoted comment, "B'ast zese bumps." Mercifully, our advent was in March, the beginning of autumn, with the dry season ahead, always my favourite time of year. As the days drew on into winter, I found the full glory of that lovely country displayed.

I have known perfection in Ireland, in England, in Scotland and am glad of each, yet here was another country, unlike anything I had ever known, possessing its own perfection in colour and line and quality. I had pictured the veld, arid, brown, vast, perhaps a little like a drought-stricken Salisbury Plain, but imagination had failed

---

[2] Bessie James Fricker who turned 100 on 5th November 1957

altogether. Vast, yes, I can imagine nothing greater, more overpowering in the feeling of infinite space, depth and height than the African night on the veld. Stepping out of the house onto the lawn after dark, into the immensity of silence and distance that seems to fill the night, as a bowl may be filled with liquid that deepens and magnifies; I have felt an awe, a wonder at the greatness of the universe, that I have known nowhere else in like measure.

I was quite unprepared for the colour of the winter veld after the first frost had come and washed out all colour with a ruthless brush. Then, as though to make amends, has with generous hand painted in from a more splendid palette, the full richness of winter colouring; the glory of reds and purples, rust and brown, so perfectly set off by the emerald of a patch of winter wheat or the bluer green of barley; by the brilliant blue of a pan or dam, and the gleaming, glittering white of distant snow-clad peaks in the sunlight.

And to this, the prodigality of colour, the beauty in line of the mountains, always visible somewhere in the picture, and the feeling of infinite distance, and there is ample compensation for all that has no place in this country. There are times when there can be a positive ache for the beech-tree, for the soft air after a day of rain, for a Dorset lane with primroses in the banks; but is it necessary to waste a day on the moors longing for a bluebell wood, or in a Cotswold beech coppice thinking of an Irish mountain? This African winter veld has its own perfection.

There is a glow that comes on the near mountains and foothills at sunset that defies description. An artist attempting to interpret faithfully that deep pink, almost luminous hillside against the far-off snow mountains, with perhaps a piece of the sky fallen into the foreground where that dam lies, would be accused of exaggeration. I may have seen it evening after evening through the winter months, yet it never failed to enchant and amaze. As the glow on the hills fades and the colour ebbs and recedes like a tide going out, there is as it were a reflection in the sky, a last reminder of all that is to be restored with the return of the morning sun. Pink fades from rich rose to a pale salmon, then yields to the lemon which in turn becomes tinged with a final promise of tomorrow's blue as though to give reassurance before the night. So at last the flow of the mountains shows up briefly in sharp contrast against a pale green wash of sky, all colour faded already from the further expanse of the heavens. Even as one watches the final radiance dims to leave illumination of that vast auditorium to the stars alone.

To me it was always sad to lose the winter colouring, welcome though the first green of spring must be, when the willows emerge, startling in their delicate freshness, like a shower of green rain caught suspended over the brown veld, its colours now spent. Yet they are fore-runners of the summer heat, and the golden lances of the poplars in autumn are the most welcome heralds. The cool clear days of March, April and May are unsurpassed, and during these months the veld puts on its winter cloak, more lovely than any summer garb.

CHAPTER 2

Decision on locality. First farm stand-in. Polo prospects

When making the decision to start farming in Africa, no particular district suggested itself at first, and it was necessary to balance up the pros and cons of as many different localities as possible before starting out in any one direction. We drew up a questionnaire and sent copies to friends in Tanganyika, Uganda, Rhodesia, Cape Province and East Griqualand; there may have been other parts, but the complete list escapes me.

The main questions of course hinged on such matters as climate for stock and growing children, educational possibilities, accessibility to suitable markets, price of land and so on. To me, one of the important points was the possibility or otherwise of keeping horses. Tse-tse areas were ruled out straight away; fortunately for me, East Griqualand, which seemed to fill the bill in every respect, and which I still consider unsurpassed as a farming proposition, had the further advantage of being a "good" horse country. There are many horse breeders in the district, and although horse-sickness is reputed to recur every seven years or so, it is by no means a scourge in East Griqualand, and inoculation appears to be a fairly efficient safeguard. On some farms, Senecio (ragwort) has bad hold, largely on overgrazed veld whence it seeds itself alarmingly. This is a real danger, for it may not have been finally proved, but it is fairly certainly established that staggers results, often after a long slow development, from Senecio poisoning. Too many horses are lost from staggers every year, there is also biliary fever resulting from tick bites, and other hazards, but precautions can be taken, and many first class polo ponies and successful racing stock have been bred in East Griqualand.

The first eighteen months in the country, we spent staying for varying periods on different farms, being unprepared as yet to take the final step and commit ourselves to the rent or purchase of a farm of our own. These months were invaluable as it was excellent experience to see the running of many different farms from the inside, to observe varying methods, to handle many natives. We were fortunate in being asked to stand in for a number of farmers in turn who took a few months leave, or had to be away for one reason or another. There was unending detail to observe, to learn, and to assess in those first months. The arts of farming, the new lore of nature, the way of the native, and the knack of improvisation, of making do, and no less of doing without, subordinating non-essentials to their proper place in the order of things, where there is so much more to be done than time in which to do it.

No day was ever long enough, but I would ride out for an hour before breakfast on one or other of the two old polo ponies on that first farm, where we took charge for eight months while the owners were in England, making sure of my ride before the day's myriad events could crowd it out. The young nephew of the house (who was the man-who-knew, while we merely supplied the support of age, *not* experience) thought me quite cracked to go riding voluntarily in the sharpness of those winter dawns, when certainly the frost, which can be as much as 20° at that altitude, 5,000 feet, could freeze my fingers to the reins. Apart from the apparent folly of riding in such cold, it was also incomprehensible to the average South African that anyone should ride for the sole pleasure of just riding and alone: as a means of getting somewhere or overseeing the work, all well and good, but only for the sake of riding, that was not understood.

To me, apart from the joy of being on a horse which never grew less, there were on these rides innumerable opportunities for observation of a hundred different aspects of my new life. I remember well the first time I discovered the fascination of a whole new volume of constantly renewing interest. Used to English roads, metalled, even when mercifully not tarmacked, I had no previous conception of the stories to be read in the thick dust of South African tracks. The print of bare feet distinct even to the lines, small feet trotting to keep up with the lengthened stride of the man with a distance to cover; the easy lope of the youth running to meet others for some single-stick contest or weekend dance, his occasional leaps in the air as he speeds on his way seen clearly in the tracks, and in imagination his arms brandishing his stick, the piece of gay material bound as a fillet round his head fluttering as he leaps. Again, the burdened woman carrying all the family possessions on her head, her baby on her back, could be read in the heavier imprint following the larger stride of the unburdened husband head. Hooves of horses, walking, trotting, cantering, tripling, plain to the eye; and the accompanying foal pausing to investigate, suddenly alarmed at the distance separating him from his dam putting on a miniature gallop, till, scattering the dust, he brings himself up short, all four feet together, across his mother's chest, causing her to falter for a moment in her stride, only to continue, apparently callous, with the small fellow once more at her quarter. It was endless pleasure to reconstruct in this way events that preceded me on the roads.

On this farm, the regular stable consisted of Benjy and George, the polo ponies, the latter an old gentleman incurably head-shy but perfectly reasonable if allowances were made for this one foible. Both were of a size conforming to the old regulations, now out of date; the banishment of any height limit has speeded up the game tremendously, but it has the disadvantage of putting first class tournament polo beyond the reach of the impoverished, where the small or average farm pony cannot hope to catch the big thoroughbred with his far superior stride. However, East Griqualand in 1937 was a wonderful country where every smallest farmer could play club polo at negligible cost; farm hacks were schooled on the farmer's daily rides around his farm, and there was a polo ground within reach of all but the most outlying farms, and even from these, where there's a will there's a way. Correct kit was by no means the bugbear it can become in England; the assortment of boots to be seen at any weekly polo day had to be seen to be believed, even old ladies' out of date hunting boots with pointed toes and tops that can only be described as bell-mouthed (what calves sometime they must have encased!) were pressed into service; and the ill-fitting breeches of every material and colour would horrify the sartorial purist; what matter as long as the game can be played.

There was no snobbery, and the complete amateur on his raw pony was given every encouragement and welcome to play with the 6, 7, and even 8 or 10 handicap players in the local community. I suppose the standard of play was as high as anywhere in the world where so little was spent on the game.

During our sojourn with George and Benjy, three other animals were added to the stable, a loan from other friends also away in England, the first proof that my horse magic had begun to work again, the magic which had started years before.

And here, I should digress and tell of those horses, which were the fore-runners of all those which came to me in South Africa in numbers I could never have imagined.

CHAPTER 3

Digression. Early mounts

From earliest pre-recollection when I have only my people's accounts to support me, I have had a great link with horses. I am told it was my custom to take a header out of my pram whenever a horse passed. The header cannot have been literal, knowing Nurse, but the attempt was all too literal, I suspect; and I am sorry for Nurse as I think of our progress through the village, for in those days a motor was a very rare monster, (conveying strange apparitions in goggles or vast enveloping veils) and horses were the rule, but perhaps the pram straps were reliable.

Bicycles for morning errands in the village were usual, although in this connection, I have visions of my mother in considerable difficulty with her hats, which were built in an age when wind-resistance and streamline were terms as yet unknown; and she would carry a sun-shade, open, on sunny days!

For family comings and goings, pony-traps, governess carts, buggies and dog-carts were the accustomed vehicles; landaus and victorias carried our grandmothers, great-aunts and cousins to their garden parties and At Homes; broughams were the rule for evening events; and I remember large family picnics when we all set forth in wagonettes. The very names of these vehicles belong to an age that is past, they strike no chord for my own children, although the British Driving Society is making them known once more.

Very early on I found threefold pleasure, horse inspired, on a day in London with my grandmother. It started with the choice of a fascinating little umbrella, having a horse's head as its handle; very cleverly carved in bone or horn. Real delight to hold and feel its curved crest fitting perfectly my small paw. Next, we took a hansom cab, still quite general in the streets of London. Trotting along in the stuffy-smelling but delightful hansom we passed ever more horses, from the huge, patient, feather-legged giant dray horses, to the sparking little ponies, put to light turn-outs or butchers' delivery-traps. Then through the Park and along beside Rotten Row, a regular galaxy of horses of every shape and size being trotted or cantered by. What a day! All the time feeling my new little horse's head, clutched safely in my hand.

Children in these days "count horses" as a pastime on long motor or bus trips, and every pony just disappearing round a corner, only a hind fetlock imaginably visible, every distant farm horse (all too few in these mechanized days) albeit a mere speck on some far-off upland, and even the "Black Horse" inn sign, (or better still, the "Coach and Horses" yielding an added bonus of four); all are pressed into service to bring the score to a respectable sum. But as a child, common though they were then, I was every bit as keen not to miss a single one, and would rush to the garden gate at every sound of passing hooves.

This passion has not faded with the years, and I have a notion that the string of horses which have come to me in such varied and unexpected ways may serve as the string on which to thread these recollections, holding together events which might otherwise fall apart, tedious to gather like scattered beads.

The very first of my string was a little chestnut mare with a white blaze, sent by my grandmother to take the family pony-trap, and to satisfy my longings for a pony to ride. Her reign was all too brief, for we were soon to move to another home, and I suppose a pony's keep became too much for the family exchequer. I shall never forget that parting and the conflicting emotions whenever we went to stay in the neighbourhood of Brownie's new home. The longing to see her battled with jealousy of her new owner. I remember the extreme discomfort of that experience of jealousy. It has left me with a horror of that soul-destroying emotion for all time. However, rather than dwell on her departure, it is pleasant to think of her arrival. I can still feel that hemp halter rope in my hand; the familiar red and blue stripes of the common halter were new to me then, and surely as glorious in that day as the trappings of any gaily caparisoned steed in the days of chivalry.

Perhaps it was as well that Brownie's stature was in no way comparable to that of the chargers of old, for my first test came on that very day of meeting. As I proudly led my pony home, pausing to display her beauty to a friend at her gates, my small foot all unwary, Brownie impatient of such delay after her journey, and equally unthoughtful of where she placed her feet, soon trod firmly on my sandal and its contents, and there her hoof remained for what seemed an eternity. I knew nothing of the technique for shifting her weight, and fearing that any protest from me might result in my having to relinquish that precious halter to grown-up hands, I preferred rather to endure the agony and hold on to this still unbelievable treasure. The imprint of that hoof stamped itself very clearly on my senses, for I was only five, and I can still see that village street and the very spot where I stood so firmly imprisoned until Brownie saw fit to take another step. This was a lesson well learnt, not only teaching me to respect a horse's feet, but also to endure uncomplainingly many discomforts, fears and hurts rather than risk interference and possible prohibition. Unthinkable to lose the chance of any ride on however unpromising a mount "because it might be too much for you". It has been good policy, well rewarded, to accept any and every mount offered, however doubtful of my own capabilities. Somehow sufficient resolution always does carry you through.

Brownie was true joy, but it was disappointing to find I was considered too little to leap on and ride off on my own; of course, I knew nothing of equitation and was quite incompetent to do any such thing, but it did not prevent me picturing it all in my imagination.

Actually, there were all the elementary stages to go through, the grind of learning to post or rise at the trot. My father would bicycle beside me, telling me he knew you had to go up and down; he must have pedalled many dusty miles as we tried to puzzle out the mysteries between us, neither knowing anything of the art. I was only allowed to ride when he could take me, and to my impatience it seemed all too seldom.

However, I soon took to driving whenever we went out in the trap, and standing up in the middle took charge like a small Boadicea in her chariot, for I could not see the road if I sat down. With what consideration I got out and walked up or down steep hills to relieve the weight of my few pounds, oblivious of the amusement it must have caused. There came an awful day when in the hands of a grown-up, Brownie was let down on her knees on a particularly steep hill. My distress for her mingled with my arrogant assumption that it was the unthinking grown-up's fault for staying in the trap and putting too much weight behind her on such a hill.

These recollections seem to point to an insufferable little creature in her pride of horsemanship, so very far from accomplished as it was. So it was all to the good, I feel sure, that Brownie soon had to go. Certainly, the long horseless years after this taught me to appreciate and make the most of any horse contact of whatever kind in the future.

There were the chargers picketed just beyond the paddock fence during manoeuvres from Salisbury Plain … later there was a grocer's pony which I discovered was game for a ride on his return from a round in the delivery cart. I would take him to his field whenever it could be achieved, and I learnt some useful lessons in careful handling as he had canker in his ears and could not bear them to be touched. Putting on the bridle required the utmost care which involved unbuckling the headpiece from the cheekpiece and placing it over with due caution; it was then I realised the value of using the voice to reassure, and the prevention of trouble by anticipation and calm handling.

Then there was a chestnut mare belonging to the local horse training establishment. In those days, each village had its own horse-breaker, for they were in constant demand. I remember the great training brakes with their high box-seats whence the trainer controlled his young animal securely shackled beside the steady old carriage horse, who could be relied on to stand like a rock in whatever emergency, and give confidence and example to his flighty young companion. This chestnut was too light a build for such a task, and was used as a steadier for young riding horses I imagine. To me she was a dream of perfection, the biggest mount to which I had attained so far. Pure bliss to be trusted to take her out alone, to look for a stubble field where I could let her go, and to bring her back gently so that she might cool down, and reach her stable in proper condition; this was the height of my joy.

An occasional word of approbation rom the old trainer sent me soaring, and I found the pleasure in proper handling, horse-management, equal to that of horse-mastership and horsemanship.

A donkey of character and the impressive name of Hildebrand contributed generously to my education in horse-mastership at about the same time. His particular occupation was to pull the bath chair of a very fine old lady, who was unable to get about by other means due to acute arthritis. She was a lady of spirit and individual character, well matched by her small grey donkey in everything but size.

There was an occasion when the old lady fell in her garden, where she loved to walk with her two sticks, accomplishing a great deal of useful weeding with the point of her stick; there was no-one within hail that day, but this did not worry her at all. Delighted to be close to the soil once more and to come to grips with the weeds at first hand at last, so far more satisfactory than at a stick's length, she got to work, and when at length discovered, she lay triumphant, the centre of the most perfectly weed-free patch in that garden, having dealt completely with every inch of ground within her not inconsiderable reach.

Realising my desperate longing, she put Hildebrand at my disposal whenever he was not wanted for her chair. He had the stubborn spirit of most donkeys, and a good deal of intelligence. I learnt a lot in my dealings with him. There was one particular lane which I avoided at all costs, for down that lane was the gate of a paddock where Hildebrand had been put to graze at some time or another. Could I prevail upon him to pass that gate? Not without long and wearisome argument and extreme patience; so if time were limited, another route had to be taken.

There was a day when I went to catch him too soon after he had been loosed in his paddock. In all probability my lack of consideration for his very real emptiness, and my own impetuous longing to be off for a ride were to blame, and Hildebrand, strong-minded donkey as he was, decided this was the time to give me a lesson. Whatever the cause, he charged me, head up, ears laid back, teeth bared. I was as much or much more hurt in my feelings that he could do such a thing to me, as frightened. However, having recovered myself to the extent of mastering my quavering voice, I found he would respond to firm tones and all was well between us, and another lesson well learnt, perhaps two.

Hildebrand trotted along very passably for a small donkey, but he saw no reason to hurry himself unduly beyond his accustomed pace. We discovered the only thing he really respected was a large broom brushing the ground behind his hind legs, this he could not bear and would put up quite a respectable canter to escape. If it were possible to get someone to cooperate and wield the broom, quite a gentle brushing behind produced the desired results. Poor Hildebrand, I do not believe he bore us any ill-will. What a lot of time and energy I expended on his thick grey donkey coat, such a different texture from that of his equine cousins. He gave a great deal of pleasure and filled an aching gap for me.

It cannot have been very long after this period when someone told me, "If you can gallop a horse round a field, you can jump." I held on to this statement, never having the chance to put it to the test, but seeing myself sailing over brush fence and timber in my imagination; many were the hunts I had from the railway carriage window with no justification whatsoever.

CHAPTER 4

Gift horse miracle

So taking every opportunity that offered, if only a cart-horse returning to his stable; with recourse to a saddle across a chair when horselessness became unendurable, I continued to send up fervent wishes on every proper occasion, the cutting of a birthday cake, a visit to a wishing well, even a wishbone, certainly there was never a more single-minded wisher. Unwavering concentration on this one great desire produced its reward in the end, for after many years, ten since the departure of Brownie, a miracle came to pass.

I have never really become accustomed to the truth of this marvel, though I had the living proof twofold under my eyes for years, yet always I could wonder and ask myself, "Can this be true?" All this is only mystifying, without further comment here is the explanation: –

One perfectly ordinary morning, as far as I could judge before I reached the breakfast table, a letter awaited me. Thereafter it became a most *extra*ordinary morning and the wonder grew from day to day.

The letter came from Lady Martin-Harvey, the wife of Sir John, the well-known actor. I knew nothing of the writer of this message from heaven, a name, no more, and I never did meet her, though we corresponded considerably. I am not even clear as to how she came to hear of me, these are unimportant details in the story of a many years' wonder. In this letter, she asked me to give a good home to her favourite hunter. She, herself, had had an operation and was no longer allowed to ride; unless she could find a perfect home for Tip-top she would have him put down, although he was then only eleven. She understood that I would give him the kind of care she would wish for him. Would I accept him?

How this proposal was discussed, and the many obstacles to the sudden acquisition of a horse disposed satisfactorily, I cannot remember clearly. The whole subject was mazed in a film of unbelievable glory. How could I keep a horse? Where? What feed would be needed, and what might pay for it? How to produce the necessary equipment? When my sole possessions in that line were Brownie's small bridle and pony saddle, neither obviously of any use for a hunter (though the saddle had done good service over that chair). I had not even a pair of breeches for myself.

A further letter from Lady M.H. presented another problem – "Tip-top has a loved companion in an old pony of mine called Joe. They have been inseparable, and I fear they will be heart-broken at being parted. If you could also do with Joe, I should be very very glad". Much as I should have loved to possess both of them, plain sense indicated "one horse just possibly, two definitely No". However, such was the generosity of my benefactor, she replied to my most regretful refusal, that she would willingly pay for keep for Joe if I would take him. Unbelievable, but so was this whole proposition. Eventually all difficulties were gradually resolved. A neighbour offered a paddock, another found a pair of irons in an attic, a third produced some leathers. An uncle sent some ancient but well-oiled pieces of tack from a long disused harness-room. I advertised the pony saddle for sale, and a small girl accompanied by a delighted grandparent arrived instantly to inspect it. They carried it off joyfully, their enthusiasm entirely compensating for the brief pang that came at the thought of losing such a cherished possession.

I was thus in the position to buy another saddle, and an ancient groom in the neighbourhood nosed out a passable object in some local loft. It met my need and my price, and all my geese were swans in those days, magically on the threshold of my miracle; but when a year later I was able to buy a saddle at a sale from nearby kennels, I realised with what an article I had made do.

Although the plan was to turn my gift horse out to grass, I could not resist the thought of a stabled hunter and a sleek head looking over half-doors. So forthwith, I got busy on the Vicarage stables, as always in those days piled to the roof with parish junk, the residue of past jumble sales, the parish bath-chair to be lent to the infirm, parish urns which played their parts at Sunday School treats, choir socials and such festivities. Somehow all this flotsam found its way to other harbourage, the coach-house after all was not figuring in my scheme as yet, though later that too played its part in housing corn bins picked up at sales; but I go on too fast; at this stage I had not aspired to oats. The thought of hay for the winter giving me quite a big enough problem to tackle for a start.

The stable cleared, a few buckets of whitewash worked wonders, and some bars turned a stall into an excellent loose-box. A cupboard in the thickness of the wall, till then obscured by junk, was transformed into a first-rate harness room, where the odd bits of leather made a brave show in my eyes. An iron saddle-tree completed the effect, and all was ready for the great day.

Impossible to convey in words the awe, the suppressed excitement, the burning expectation with which I went to the station to meet the horse-box announced by Lady M.H., whatever old screw it might have transported would have been wonder enough, anything on four legs would have brought me joy. When that truck was eventually shunted into the siding and the side unbarred and let down, it was not possible to believe in the glory within. I just moved in a dream and prayed I need not wake up. I have often been asked to tell the story of my first horse, and that dream quality still holds through every repetition; I never became accustomed to it, always there was that magic aura, it never lost its charm. But in those first hours I was floating in it, suspended in a mist of unbelievable delight.

The partitions were up and at first all that could be seen were shapely legs, far more shapely than any I had dared imagine. The last barrier down, out came a 15.2 bay, full of quality and no little spirit, snorting and snatching at his rope. While I restrained him, the station staff were busy with the next partition, and in a few moments yet one more miracle took form in the composed and immediately self-confident rounded figure of a pure white pony, 12 hands or so, mane and tale and general demeanour worthy of any circus, a character as could be seen at a glance. Joe, I had learnt, was getting on in years, but still game to do odd garden jobs, or even carry children.

Then ensued a triumphal procession through the streets of that country town; a friend leading Joe, an immediate draw to all the youth of the place; myself still dazed at Tip-top's head, as he curvetted on the tarmac and showed his impatience at his late confinement, and at the same time his undoubted breeding.

Too good to be true that such perfection should be mine, yet true it was; and as Cinderella's fairy godmother left no detail unprovided, so mine heaped glory upon glory. As though it were not enough to bring me a pair of animals of such quality, that horse-box carried also a horse rug and good (undreamed of luxury, surely only worn by the highest aristocracy of the equine world), a leather headcollar, such as I had often coveted in saddlers' windows in the past, and sundry articles of grooming kit, bandages and the like, which spoke of stabling to which my steed had been accustomed. By that time nothing could add to the maze in which I moved, it was all beyond belief.

So the magic began, and once started, it went on, somehow, Tip led the way and others followed, for since that day when I unboxed my very first gift horse, it has fallen to me to meet many others; sometimes they have come as Tip-top did by train, and I have never failed to find the same excitement as I watch the bars come down, and get my first, always delighted, glimpse of a set of limbs. Not always so shapely as those of Tip's, for he was indeed as near perfection as one could wish or hope, yet there was joy in each and every animal it has been my great good fortune to possess.

Tip-top and Joseph set the ball rolling, I was eighteen when they came to me. In the next 27 years no less than eleven horses were given to me outright, and I have had sole use of 25 others, for varying periods from a few months to several years at no cost whatever. With each one I had to pinch myself again and ask, "Can it be true?"

The advent of Tip and Joe was an excitement to the neighbourhood, they held court in their paddock the first Sunday after their arrival, when after church the whole congregation appeared to find its way home past their gate. It was not long before kind friends suggested I should give riding lessons on Joe to their children, thereby earning enough to buy oats for Tip-top, that he might hold the necessary condition to carry me hunting. How I had the face to take these children, when I knew little enough myself, I cannot see now. I suppose my longing to hunt blinded me to the obvious effrontery of such a pretension.

Fortunately Joe would keep his nose glued to Tip's quarter, and I could always rely on his immediate response to any aid I gave to Tip; so I had no need to trouble about controlling Joe; to control Tip was enough, and all my spare faculties might be concentrated on keeping Joe's small rider in the saddle. What I taught these children, I often wonder now, it was a case of learn as you go for me, and I was having my first chance to put into practice the mass of theory I had collected from reading every book on Horsemanship on which I could lay my hands.

CHAPTER 5

First hunt. End of Tip-Top

The ignorance and inexperience with which I set out for my first day's hunting was past belief. Here again, how had I the cheek to go at all without guide or counsellor? When I had read enough to realise there would be many pitfalls, many blunders against etiquette, which I should be liable to make, all uninitiated as I was.

Added to these terrors of social procedure, which loomed large as I looked at the grand cavalry gentlemen at the Meet in their immaculate swallow-tails, there were very real fears as to my own proficiency. Should I ever get across country in company with Tip, and remain united? I meant to have a try at it, but could not help doubting my ability, for I had never been over a fence as yet, and had little confidence. Thinking it over now, I cannot imagine why I never managed to put up some sort of pile of brushwood, fallen branch or obstacle of any kind to test my own and Tip's powers a little before we had to perform in public as it were. The only reason seems to have been that I had no suitable ground on which to practise. That first paddock I remember was all on a steep slope, there was no level bit anywhere to put a jump, and I had not then been able to explore sufficiently to find common ground where I might contrive an obstacle.

Anyway, I suppose I was too impatient; to hunt had been my ambition as long as I could remember; here was my hunter, therefore, why wait any longer?

I found Tip-top just as keen to go as I was myself; he had not seen hounds for a few years I had gathered, indeed, Lady M.H. had warned me – "He may be a bit fresh for a time or two" – this was putting it mildly, and as long as he was with me, he never failed to be more than "a bit fresh" whenever hunting was in the air.

As we drew near the Meet, and horses passed us in ones and twos, up went Tip's head and he began to dance, this was something he knew, I might be ignorant but not so Tip. I soon realised that Tip on his own was a very different proposition from Tip in company, and he had been quite exciting enough alone. It became very evident I should have all my work cut out to hold him at all. When hounds came round the corner, he and I had to remove ourselves to the outskirts of the crowd for fear of creating too much disturbance.

I decided to keep behind for my first hunt and watch what other people did, then I need not fear committing some frightful crime in ignorance. Unfortunately, Tip-top did not share my views in this respect, he was all for seeing things from the front. The mingled joy and fear, real abject fear, of that day I shall not forget. It was sheer joy to be there, something I had dreamed of for years, not daring to hope it might come true, actually out with the hunt on my horse.

There was the whole magic of the scene, the pageantry of hounds and scarlet coats, shining bays and chestnuts and blacks, spectacular greys; the thrill that never fails to uplift at the sight of spirit, courage, breeding, quality in that noblest animal of all; the smell of English autumn's soft, moist air, of horse and leather and soil; the colour at the covertside, from the autumn woods at hand, to the blue distant hills across the patterned vale, all set off by the moving splashes of scarlet, white and black and tan. The thud of hooves on the turf, or squelch in the lanes and bridle-paths, the snort and jingle, and the creak of saddle leather, the music of hounds and the sound of the horn, which sets hearts of men leaping; all this makes up a combination of scene, of scent, of sound that is unique and unsurpassed. It is this quality, so many perfections appealing to all the senses simultaneously, that makes hunting excel.

When I was playing polo, I could not think that any other horse activity could approach it for thrill, speed, art and delight in horsemanship; yet it is only necessary to recreate for a moment any hunting morning, and I know that there is the height of experience. It worked its spell on me that first day, for despite my fears, social and physical, and the shocking exhibition I made of myself, I was never able to resist going out on every occasion that offered itself, still frightened, and still bewitched.

Tip-top and I kept modestly in the rear as we moved off, not without considerable effort on my part to restrain, and on Tip's to get, his head. So we fought our way to the first covert, and somehow remained together as we waited more than impatiently (I speak for Tip) to get going. With the "gone away", Tip took the law into his own hands, and the bit between his teeth. All my intentions went to the winds, and we galloped with the best of them. For a field or two, all was fairly well, we were in the main rush and inconspicuous, and despite the very painful realisation that I was out of control, I could not but feel the thrill, besides, Tip was loving it.

However, I soon met my Waterloo, a wired-up fence, only a narrow gap to jump, the field playing follow my leader. I should have liked to be a coward and wait my turn at the end of the line, with few eyes to watch my untutored seat over a jump, and maybe a somewhat lowered obstacle to negotiate. Tip had other ideas, and caring nothing for etiquette, he saw no reason why he should wait his turn; he plunged through the affronted throng, scattering cursing stalwarts to right and left, and took off with a colossal leap under the patrician noses of a couple of the cavalry brigade. Whether it was sheer incompetence, or partly because I was still battling to get hold of Tip, and probably sitting down too hard in the attempt, whatever the cause, as Tip soared into the air, I soared higher, and coming down an appreciable time later, it seemed, met, not the saddle but the turf. I still had hold of the reins and Tip dragged me the whole length of that field by the reins alone. When eventually I stopped him, the rim of my bowler was cracked irrevocably, it gradually disintegrated during the day and dropped off; my back was plastered with Wiltshire mud. I was soon in the saddle again, and much comforted when one of the superior gentlemen actually said something kind about it being a good show not to lose my horse. Probably they were none of them so superior as I imagined. It was only in my extremity of alarm that everyone, being so vastly more competent in every way, seemed likely to despise my efforts. I know now of course they were unlikely to think about me at all.

Tip and I were both sobered after this display, and we managed to keep ourselves in a more modest position thereafter, and got through the day without encountering anything very alarming.

Finally, we found ourselves hacking home, both aching and weary, but blissfully happy, except for a haunting thought in my mind that I should never know when I might soar in the air over another fence and fail to make contact again. "Sufficient unto the day," however, and it had been indeed an all-sufficing day.

As I rode through the streets of that country town, the same which had seen the triumphal procession of Tip and Joe on their arrival, I passed members of the Mothers' Meeting going to their "social", and heard comments on the state of my bowler and my back. I waved at them gaily so they could see that my limbs were more or less intact, for they were sure to carry vivid accounts to my parent whom they would be meeting.

A couple of hours hard work in the stable by lantern light saw Tip bedded down, ragged and bandaged, he had had warm gruel on coming in, and later a linseed mash, which I had left simmering before I started for the meet. I so hoped he did not miss his grand stable and experienced groom too badly. All I did had to come out of books; there was plenty of enthusiasm, and very, very little real knowledge. I committed fearful crimes such as once plaiting Tip-s mane with coloured tapes for hunting, as though for a carthorse show! But the joy he gave me was immeasurable, and I learnt perhaps the most important lesson of all, that there is never an end to learning in horsemanship and horsemastership. Tip must have been wonderfully long-suffering, but then horses are so amazingly generous; what he bore with my unskilled handling and grooming, I hate to think. Only once did his feelings get the better of him for a moment. I was working away at an obstinate patch of mud in a particularly ticklish place on the inside of his thigh. It became unbearable, and Tip whipped his head round and took hold of a mouthful of muscle in the middle of my back, bent double as I was in my ministrations. I spoke to him and instantly he let go, and plunged into the corner of his box, quivering all over, his head high in the air, every nerve taut, prepared for the punishment he obviously expected. When I went to his head and apologised for my own mishandling, he could hardly believe it; perhaps that efficient groom to whom I had always felt so inferior, had had a like experience and responded differently. Tip seemed really overcome with remorse, he nudged me reassuringly and thereafter never once repeated his mistake.

Many times he had to bear that unendurable dealing with his tender bits, but he found he could relieve his feelings by hanging on to the manger with every evidence of fury, ears laid back, teeth bared, but always he would make things right at the end with that comforting nudge.

Joseph, on the other hand, showed his individuality by getting in deliberate nips on my person through the bars, as I laboured on Tip's toilet with my back to the next stall. He stayed out in a paddock all day, while Tip was kept in altogether during the hunting season. (I had made friends with a farmer, who let me have oats at a very kind price, and riding pupils paid for them), but Joe came in at night to give Tip the benefit of his companionship, and he soon found how to walk out of his paddock whenever he felt inclined for company. He would stroll up the garden path, pull the bolt of the stable door with his lips, and take himself in. Fortunately, Tip's box was made from the inside stall and his bars were even proof against Joe. Frequently, he would bring himself in for a chat while I was grooming Tip, and would stand in his stall looking as if butter would not melt in his mouth; just to enliven matters as I said, he would take an occasional very harmless nip at my anatomy, but always before I could turn round to upbraid him, he had resumed his accustomed innocent expression. You could only laugh at him.

During the summer, when the two of them were out at grass together, from time to time I would be summoned to catch my horses that had got out. Invariably it was Joseph who had crawled through a gap, even contriving to ease himself under quite low wire, and having got himself to the far side of the fence, he would neigh to Tip to follow him. Tip would then jump out, a thing he would never do on his own, but they were a very satisfactory pair to own.

For six years they were mine, three seasons hunting Tip gave me, then I found myself working in London, and Tip and Joe waited for me at grass in the care of that oat-providing farmer. At the end of the slum period, my marriage made it impossible to keep horses. Joe had definite signs of ringbone, and his age being considerable, I decided it was safer to put him down for fear he should be worked by people who did not realise he was unfit for it. So, having written to Lady Martin-Harvey, whom I had kept informed from time to time of the well-being of her friends, I arranged for him to go.

Tip-top was a problem, for I had promised when he came to me that I would never part with him, but see that he came to a happy end if I could no longer keep him. He was still so young in spirit, so gay and full of life, I could not bear to let him go then with Joe. There was always the faint hope that someday I might be in a position to have him again.

Accordingly with his first owner's permission, I lent him to a girl of whom I had heard, who apparently was in much the same position as I had been in myself when Tip-top came; longing for a horse and caring enough to look after him herself. The only stipulation was that, should she find it impossible to keep him at any time, she would let me know at once. And as Tip's life had been a miracle, so surely his end was of the same nature.

There came a time when his temporary owner had to go abroad; she wrote that she would have to send him back to me. I was in no position to keep a horse, and realised I must now let him go the way Joes had preceded him, but I must just see him again. Immediately, the magic began to work; we were in the North, my old home was in the South, we were due for leave the very week Tip must be sent back. So I asked that he should return to his old home, and the same farmer gave him grazing in the same old paddock, which he had shared with Joe. I was at the station to meet him, and lived through that first arrival once again, as the horse box shunted into that same siding. The same thrill as the side went down, but this time there was a greeting from an old friend as he nickered to me before the partition could be removed; and in a moment, the old friendly nudge that had often nearly pushed me into a hedge with its fervour. But he was as young as ever, it seemed, and he pulled me all through those familiar streets on the end of his halter rope, so keen to be back in his old field. It was glory to see him canter round, snorting and blowing, smelling out all his well-known corners, and then flinging a final buck of delight he came galloping back to me, putting on four-wheel brakes at the gate to come skidding and sliding to my side for that bit of carrot he knew he could expect. Forget? Not he, not a detail.

A fortnight we had together, and the only blot was the thought of what must come at the end of this time. I did not know how to bring myself to make that final move. Seeing Tip so gay and splendid, it seemed impossible to face, yet I knew the end had got to come, but postponed it as long as I dared. I need not have worried; the magic was still working. The last day before I must act, the farmer rang up, would I come up to the field. There lay Tip perfectly at ease, he had been cantering round, his old self, and his end came so easily there in his old field, saving me all sad decisions, taking him sure in the care of his friends. A post-mortem revealed a clot that had reached his heart, this the scientific explanation of a miracle.

CHAPTER 6

Army chargers. Lady J

The parting with Tip-top completed an Act, and there was an interlude before the next in my string of gift horses came on the scenes. I was fortunate in having the use of all the Regimental chargers for hacking on the Yorkshire moors, where we were stationed at the time: each with its own individual characteristics.

Hussar, quite a well-made compact type, up to weight, with plenty of spirit, so that he needed riding.

Dragoon, somewhat of a weed, slab-sided, without the substance to promise well for long days campaigning, but beloved by the grooms for he repaid their work, taking the eye with his shining coat and imagined blood lines – an easy ride and always ready to go.

Sir Toby, big and bony and bay, a pleasant fellow, the sort to chaff, he would never do anything spectacular, but he would carry you for a day's hunting, and somehow get there, as much to his own surprise as his rider's.

Then there was a mare, never distinguished by a name, except among the grooms, who had their own names, she was probably Mabel or something equally unsuitable, for they seemed to look to their lady friends for inspiration in these matters. She was just known as C. Coy: charger, and looked at with suspicion by most of the Battalion as she was tricky, could throw the odd buck when least expected, and needed careful handling; she was a good type and showed signs of quality.

Little fat Susan, coveted by those who wanted a safe, comfortable ride, shared an adventure with me on the high moors. Her nature tuned in with the genial lines of her rounded form, which must have helped on this occasion. In the end, but it may be that she lacked the instinctive wisdom of most of her kind, and that her comfortable, easy-going outlook dulled her sharper perceptions, or simply that she was not country-bred, and bogs were outside her scope. However it was, she and I crossing the moor both failed to notice the treacherous green of a patch of bog: one step and before there was time to realise it, we were in over the saddle flaps, and I felt the wet through my breeches.

Fortunately, the bog patch was not wide in area, I just managed to kick my feet free and spring on to a tuft which held, mercifully. I had firm hold of the reins, and encouraged the terrified Susan, whose frantic plunges promised only to send her deeper into the bog. Luckily she listened to my voice as I tried to calm her, and, pulling her head hard towards solid ground, she got a forefoot onto an unyielding tussock, encouragement and gentle ear-pulling helped her to make the final effort, she staggered clear and stood trembling. I was afraid she might have strained herself, so took her very quietly back as soon as she had got over the first effects of shock. Poor girl, it had shaken her, but she was none the worse, and I doubt whether she ever set foot in a bog again.

Two of these chargers made their very special mark on my own experience. One, a brown mare, Moira, from Ireland, who carried me for two wonderful seasons with the Shortcliff Drag two days a week; she never put a foot wrong, and covered up all my incompetence with her own high courage. She would take me to the front at the very first fence and keep me there, well away from the mob which constituted the chief danger; for other people out of control, jumping across in a narrow place, or coming down under your nose, were frequently the cause of disaster. I never knew Moira to hesitate or think of refusing, she carried me sublimely, and on her back I began to think I knew something about jumping, but it was all her; if you know your horse won't think of refusing, it is easy to be in the right place. There was even a wonderful day when a gate at the end of a line was found padlocked, the Master and the Whip both refused and turned to see Moira behind them. Asked if my mare could give them a lead, I could only say I would try it, and left it all to her.

She was another example of that truly great generosity of nature, the rule among horses, the exception, alas, among humans.

At the same time, there was another mare in the Regimental stables, but in the draught lines, where obviously the animals were of heavier build. Indeed, many were real hairy heels, though the actual feather was not to be seen owing to frequent clipping and trimming. This one chestnut mare took the eye as one walked through the line, as she was obviously of lighter build and showed more quality, and although as I have said, all were trimmed alike, it was easy to see her fetlocks would not belie her. It seemed a pity she should not come into the other more aristocratic side of the stable among the chargers, if her performance was up to her promise.

The transport officer in charge of all horses, gave his permission that she might be tried out, but was obviously not sanguine. Going to the stables to start out on my ride I found a skull and crossbones painted over her stall; this looked ominous and the grooms explained she would savage them or use her heels when they went into her stall. Accordingly, no-one approached her without the protection of a pitchfork, and, as I discovered, often shouted threats. Probably herein lay the reason for her banishment to the draught lines, no-one had thought it worthwhile going further with an animal of such reputation. She could show the whites of her eyes like most chestnuts, but she did not look a real rogue. Anyway, I had planned to try her, so with grooms at her head and my stirrup, I mounted and rode quietly out of barracks, determined to get right away into the country on my own, and try to get on terms with her.

She carried me quietly enough, but I could feel the quiver under me, and from the flick of an ear and the rolling of an eye knew she was trying to take my measure. We were each uncertain of the other, and I sympathized with her feeling, for I was secretly in a funk, wondering what I might be in for, and she must have been wondering just as much what she might expect from me. She was right on her toes, shivering, and I had a job to keep the quaver out of my voice. Still, it had to be done, I should not stand a chance if I did not put the fear right under. So as we walked apparently sedately, I hoped, out of barracks, I talked to her quietly all the way, put a hand on her shoulder from time to time, tried to establish confidence. The quiver died away, the nervous flick of the ears gave way to careful listening, one ear back to my voice, one forward to the job in hand carrying me out into the country.

So, we gradually got on terms, she showed me her paces, and I found she had a perfect snaffle mouth. When I judged we were sufficiently far away to be certain of no disturbance, I dismounted, not without a momentary wonder, what if she would not allow me to mount without someone at her head? Had she always been held down? However, she would not be much use if she could not get over that anyway, so it had to be put to the test. She had appeared to be putting up with me fairly well in the saddle, how should we be face to face?

She was obviously suspicious and ran back the length of her reins, but what could one expect knowing she had always been approached with pitchforks and threats? Luckily, she had become accustomed to my voice already, so a bit of quiet talking enabled me to shorten the distance between us. I had provided my pockets with an assortment of carrot, apple, even sugar, hoping to find something she liked. There was a deal of snorting and blowing before she would come close enough to savour the offering, the first pieces I tried were blown away with these distrustful blasts; but there was plenty of time. After a bit, I just left her all the slack of the rein and sat on the grass – very gently and talking all the time – for any sudden move of mine might have set her off, and if I once let go of those reins, well that would have been that, I suppose. Fortunately, the manoeuvre worked, she blew great snorts down the back of my neck, and was more suspicious than ever for a time, but I kept on talking, she kept on blowing, until little by little the snorts became less and eventually, there she was, cropping beside me, not quite peacefully perhaps, for she would raise her head anxiously every few bites, but it was at least a beginning. Then I tried again with my bits of carrot, gently advancing a hand near where she was cropping. Victory at last, she took a piece, found it good, another, till at last she even took a step nearer me to get more; this was splendid, and we got to know each other much better.

Eventually, still talking, I was able to stand beside her, give more carrot and scratch her neck with the hand that held the reins. After that, there was no more trouble, she had accepted me; she listened as I told her to stand for me to mount and we turned for home with a glorious feeling or companionship in place of that first suspicion. I felt she enjoyed the canter back across the downs as much as I did; it was with no pretended calm that we walked into barracks, it was with real quiet assurance that we returned. Thus it was the simplest thing in the world to slip from her back at the stable door, give her neck another scratch, and signing the groom aside, lead her into her stall, and under the skull and crossbones give her a last piece of carrot.

After that I went in and out of her stall any time I was near the stables, and it was arranged that an excellent groom looked after her, who was unafraid. She was no longer threatened, so soon forgot to expect to have to defend herself. She was moved into the charger stables, and the sign over her manger did not move with her.

The groom told me her name was Joyce, but she was known as the Killer. The latter name dropped away from her quite naturally. I could not share their taste for girlish names, so rechristened her Lady J. for my own benefit. She became a grand mare with the Drag, and even ran in a point-to-point, going well always in a snaffle. Her style was not so perfect as Moira's over the fences, but she had a great heart, and went with the best. She had a big head with a suspicion of a Roman nose, and was inclined to look a bit gaunt at the end of the season, but she was hard and sound, and one of the best loved of all. In the end, no-one thought twice about going into her stall. She lived down that earlier reputation completely.

How lucky we were to have had our time with the Army in the days when there were still officers' chargers, and fifteen bobbers to be had from the Cavalry during the hunting season. Very soon after we retired to farm in South Africa, mechanization wiped out the last remaining horses in the Infantry regiments, and it is now a very different life, certainly for impoverished wives.

CHAPTER 7

Moods and nostalgic thought

Thinking back, I realise how much Tip-top and Joe gave me, even beyond the initiation of the veritable string that followed in due time. On Tip's back, I felt free of the woods and fields, he saved me from being an intruder, his hoof on the fallen leaves of autumn was no encroachment, from his saddle I could watch the wild things – a heron by the water's edge, a hare on the upland, or an owl at dusk off for his evening hunt – and find them unafraid. He could give me the freedom of the wind as we galloped on the downs, and always that companionship of understanding and trust so generously given.

With him, I found release from hampering moods. We could put distance between ourselves and all that chafed, and in the peace of the country let go the weights that dragged. We could reach places sufficiently remote to allow me to declaim aloud from the repertoire I had gradually built up, having formed the habit of memorizing poems since early days. A very useful store on many occasions when sleep evades, or depressing thoughts persist.

There was a gradual progression from earliest recollection of reciting "The Lady of the Lake" in the bath, glorying in the acoustics as the rhythms rolled round the room gaining resonance from the depth of water in the bath.

"The stag at eve had drunk his fill, where danced the moon on Monan's rill, And deep his midnight lair had made in lone Glenartney's hazel shade."

The picture conjured from these lines appealed to all my tastes, the sound of words, the feeling of wild country, and the glory of the chase. Thence through Newbolt, "He climbed alone to the eastward edge of the trees, all night long in a dream untroubled of hope he brooded clasping his knees" – Drinkwater, "Deep in the summer night my Cotswold hill aslant my window sleeps" – Keats, "In some melodious plot of beechen green and shadows numberless..." – Houseman, "Loveliest of trees, the cherry now is white with blossom on the bough..." – Thus, onto the Shakespeare sonnets (several more of these acquired as I walked up and down a South African cowshed during milking).

All this very salutary, Tip must have set free many of the repressions common to youth. He introduced me to much of true value, such as the old blacksmith, one of the real craftsmen. There had been smiths in his family for generations, as his name bore testimony. It was good to see his smile of pleasure as he brought out the set of shoes made ready, knowing it must be about time we should be along, and his delight in the good shape of Tip's feet.

Always the country has brought satisfaction. I remember early visits to Ireland, where the enchantment never fails. It is in the softness of the air, the cadence of the voices of her people, the blues and greens of her mountains and hills, purple too, colours that can be found nowhere else on earth. It is in the great banks and grey walls, the white cabins, and the black shawls of the women, and in their grey eyes. Again, in the little grey and brown donkeys and jennets, and in the bogs with their many shades – the black bog water, the dark rich brown of the turf, changing colour as it dries. Above all it is in the smell, which has in it all the sweetness of the Irish air, wind, heather, turf, and the very fragrance of the burning, which is prophecy.

There are Scottish mountains too, proud and grand, always changing as you watch, great shadows fleet across, and sunlight paints vivid pictures on their rocks. Some catch wisps of cloud on their reaching summits, they are rich with the colour of the heather, and in the distance, there is blue of glorious depth.

Where I stayed there is a yew avenue with deep shadows and twisting trunks, sometimes an arrow of light pierces the shade making sudden patterns on the sombre ground. Some days the loch was like pewter, and I remember one small bay that was an old looking-glass when it has become blurred and dim, a lovely elusive grey, reflecting vague shadowy forms. With these memories there returns a day of rain, when I climbed through a quiet wood, treading silently on moss that spread richly under my feet, a brilliant radiant green; under branches of feathery larch, through red-brown trunks of pines, beneath the blue-green of firs. On and up I went, past bracken showing a promise here and there of gold, and once a vivid patch of orange fungus among the moss, all washed and fresh with the rain which fell gently, spreading a faint grey veil over all; not obscuring but somehow enhancing the colours with a touch of mystery. There was silence full of sound, the pattering of the rain on the leaves, the hundred little noises of the wood, the drip of raindrops into moss.

Then suddenly, the trees were behind, and I was out on the mountain above the wood, and all around was purple moor and grey rain. Lying on the wet heather, I could feel the drops steal down into the very heart of the hillside, and in that stillness, there was perfect beauty of sight and sound and feeling. There quite close was a brown burn trickling, and on my way down, a great white owl flew from a dark fir tree.

These are among the things that last; indeed, looking back at these early memories with the enlightened eyes of a septuagenarian, I see the essence of all that has really counted in all my experience. The happiness in those first village days has lasted, because there were all the elements which have proved of abiding value. Understanding companionship, perfect trust and love, books and the country, the close link with animals, which has always brought joy, and that spiritual treasure, not apprehended fully, yet bringing perhaps not content, yet the unformed realisation that Good is one with Beauty, so that there I sought and found release. As Beauty is Truth, so surely, I had touched the ultimate values all unknowing, but then I had no need to know.

CHAPTER 8

Slums interlude

There was a recurring dream of horror which found me in the toils of city life and the evil embodied there. The black despair and paralysing misery which took hold in those surroundings still cast their shadows when I am cut off from real country for a time, but they have lost their power, which used to be strong and crushing. Travelling to London by train as a very small child, the sordid, soot and smoke-blackened tenement buildings, backing on the line as it approaches Paddington, made an impression on me which was like a threat from some inhuman evil ogre. I saw the slatternly women hanging their grimy pathetic shreds of washing from filthy windows, with listless grubby arms, defeated from the start, and I wondered how they could go on from day to day.

As I went through the streets of London, I looked in the faces of the people and saw the despair, the utter lack of hope, and sensed that what I saw was bred in the city. The fear of that ogre haunted me awake and asleep until I discovered the only way to get on terms with that anguish, as with all others – to accept.

I believe now that there is no escape from any fear, any pain, any grief, until one has learnt to accept. Face it, take what has to be borne, and the burden is eased, the load lightened and finally comes release. It can be found in no other way. This is the theme of that play "The Giaconda Smile", adapted from Aldous Huxley's story. So it was only when I went to London deliberately to live (because I had so dreaded ever having to stay there, feeling it would be physically and mentally impossible) and worked among the people of those slums, who formerly had filled me with so much horror, that I eventually escaped from the power of that evil. Considering the plight of these unfortunates, doomed to live out their days without the healing of the country, the only way to reach any peace of mind was to undertake to work among them. It was little enough, but to put even a few unhappy depressed prisoners of circumstance in touch with the means of partial relief; to find a family of seven, in two rooms at the top of a flight of rickety stairs, their only water a tap in the yard, their slops in a bucket on the precarious landing, the mother far gone with consumption, the children dangerously exposed in that confined space, where two or three at least must sleep in the room with the consumptive, and to be able to send the woman to a good sanatorium, the children to homes where they could be watched for early signs of the disease, and where conditions would help them to fight it, should it have taken hold already – these small achievements helped towards a more balanced view of city life. The frequent instances of light relief perhaps completed the cure.

There was the queer old "quack" with his very doubtful practice in a back street, his Irish brogue, his whisky fumes, yet his real kindliness and understanding of these people, whom he did so much to help in his rough and blasphemous way. I sat on a bench among the patients, taking my turn for an interview, when only with an effort at supreme tact I wheedled out of him some essential information for one of my cases, and as I left he shouted after me he was between the devil and a burning fiery furnace, more terrible than any deep blue sea. This in his rich Irish, and a mighty roar raised a laugh even among those sad victims of pain, poverty, depression and dire need. Was I the devil or the fiery furnace, I wondered, but there was no ill-feeling.

Often, I was looked on with deep suspicion, usually the door was opened but a crack, and sometimes a deftly inserted toe the only means of keeping it open long enough to allow me to break down the defences and establish confidence. Certainly, I felt every sympathy with them, and found it most understandable that they should resent my intrusion; I felt most horribly nosey, and hated having to pry into their affairs.

These people did far more for me than I ever even pretended to do for them. Wonderful kindliness and good nature, self-sacrifice, uncomplaining slavery, and high-hearted courage I found behind those blackened, sordid walls, that had so depressed my earliest journey. The shadow remains, but there is no shadow without sun. "Ut umbra sic vita."

CHAPTER 9

Final hunts. Prophet's Thumb. Native ponies

There had been a couple of years in England between the army charger period and the departure for South Africa, when the ages of my small children, and the lack of horses in the neighbourhood, had combined to prevent any but very infrequent horse activity. However, my kind brother had given me three never to be forgotten hunts, shortly before I left England, He himself later showed considerable ingenuity in getting rides in unpromising circumstances; he found a horse somehow during the Libyan campaign, trained it on the edge of the desert, finally borrowed a baker's van and, turning it into a horse-box trailer, conveyed the animal a hundred miles or so for a race meeting. This particular horse had no luck, I believe, though he ran well, but one thing leads to another, and, having been spotted in that race, he was offered a mount in a later event, which he won.

He had arrived on leave from India, luckily for me, in the nick of time before I was due to set off for my farming future. In his usual way he planned immediately how to give me the greatest treat I could imagine. One day with the Cattistock with him, and two in my old country, the Avon Vale left me with a flavour I shall never forget. I had a different mount for each of these hunts, but he had hired for me with such particular care that each one carried me to glory, and I mean that in the literal sense, and not in the accepted colloquial one!

They must, all three, have been artists, for they covered up successfully my own bad riding, and took my creaking bones over the country in safety, despite my usual apprehension, added to the fact that I had not touched a saddle for two years. One, in particular, I remember as a mare of exceptional talent, one of the cleverest I have ever known, and on her I saw for the first time the Prophet's thumb mark, or the Thumb of Allah.

I believe this indentation in thickness of the muscle in the neck, goes by a variety of names, but it is said that only an exceptionally good horse ever shows it. A superstition of course, but certainly the only two I have ridden myself, bearing this mark, have been quite outstanding in performance, courage and wisdom. It is said that some tribes value animals thus marked so highly, that they are only purchased by sums apparently quite disproportionate to their intrinsic value. I should be interested to hear more of the subject. There must be legends attached, and probably different countries have their own versions.

I found no recognition of this mark among the Africans in East Griqualand where we farmed, but these natives show no true love of the horse in their make-up. They almost all possess one or two poor skinny ill-made animals, on which they get about the country, but they seem to appreciate them for their use alone. They do set store by an animal that might win a race at their Sunday meetings, even these are often very poor specimens, weeds with a turn of speed perhaps, but no stamina apparent to the eye, though perhaps I malign the poor wretched creatures, for stamina of a kind they must have to subsist somehow on the bare frosted veld grass throughout the winter, dragging themselves about when they look nothing but a bag of bones, even in this state shaking themselves into a shambling canter to carry their masters to the local beer drink on a Sunday night.

Certainly, a boy working on a farm will take many an odd bit of illicit feed to give his poor beast if he sees the chance, and the animals fancied as race horses somehow get a surprising amount of grain when it is all too scarce in the boss's stable. But it is usually given, it appears, for what can be got out of the animal subsequently, either in racing, or as a more rapid means of transport, than for any feeling of care for the pony's well-being on his own account. There are exceptions of course, but this is the general tendency.

There is an excellent type of sturdy pony that comes originally from Basutoland, sure-footed, used to the precipitous country and rough going of those parts, and up to a surprising amount of weight for his not very considerable stature, carrying the large-framed European and his saddlebags for long distances, showing undoubted stamina. There are, however, not many of the true type to be seen in East Griqualand. The native ponies have sadly deteriorated, and although you may see here and there a Basuto type, it is usually all too obviously much crossed with the indiscriminate native pony. The Africans, by their careless habits leaving young colts ungelded indiscriminately among the mares, have weakened the stock shockingly, and the general level is low.

Occasionally a thoroughbred cross is obvious among them, a cast-off polo pony mare perhaps, sold to a boy and bred to the casual native stallion in the bunch. Or sometimes a boy puts his own mare to the white man's thoroughbred. In a group of native ponies, therefore, there are from time to time good lines to be seen, a rare flash of quality, but it is the exception; on the whole they are unpleasing to the eye, and too often pathetic in the extreme.

Tip's influence was to follow me to South Africa. Indeed, it was there that the charm really started working overtime, and horses began to come to me by ones and twos, till one day I counted up my stud, and found it numbered no less than thirteen, and I had never then paid a single penny for a horse. Of course, they were not all my own, but I had the use of every one of them, what more could I want? I had also attained my ambition to breed for myself, and to break in and train young ones from the start.

CHAPTER 10

Early days. Guest house horses. Mount Currie ride.

We spent eight months on the first farm, where Benjy and George were mounts, and Con, Mary, Pip and the foal (those three on loan had increased to four with the advent of the latter) gave all the horse interest possible. Then our hosts returned from England, and still being farmless ourselves, we moved to a succession of farms, where for periods varying from a fortnight to two or three months, we took charge during the owners' absences on holiday, sick leave, or for other reasons.

There was a time when I found myself parked with the children at a guest-farm, a place where townsfolk from Durban or elsewhere came up to the cooler heights of East Griqualand to escape the heat below. Here I found a motley collection of typical native ponies for guests to ride. They were poor in quality and spirit; no-one gave them a thought save to order them round to the door if a visitor wanted a ride. I discovered the saddlery without exception was ill-fitting and worse adjusted, hooves needed trimming, girth-galls and saddle sores required healing. Somehow the stable was handed over to me to run, and at least there was some satisfaction in sending out an animal with a bridle that fitted, the bit in the right place in its mouth, the girth untwisted, and sores healed. But they were a sorry crew, rejoicing in such names as Heather, Dawn, Black Bess.

I discovered a grey weed of a stallion in the paddock, supposed to be only half trained, so not in demand for daily rides. Poor fellow, he should never have been left ungelded, but he gave me many rides as he was always available, and being a stallion had slightly more spirit than his unhappy mates.

Seeing me riding this animal, I suppose, a neighbouring farmer asked me to take out his stallion, a bay called Challenger. He had little more right to have been left entire, but he was certainly a step up both in quality and condition, and gave me some fun.

It was from this contact that I came in for an amusing episode. A farmer nearby told me how a strange white man had turned up at his farm some four months back, apparently trekking on horseback, though he had been very reticent about his doings or intentions. Indeed, he was in no state to converse at all. He appeared to have had a fall, and had hurt his back; he could not even dismount. They had lifted him down and taken him to hospital, keeping his horse on the farm. The whole thing was a mystery, as they heard no more from him at all, and were not even informed when he left hospital, or where he had gone.

However, a letter had just come to tell them he would be fetching his horse shortly, would they have it exercised, as of course it would be soft after all those months, and in no condition to face another long trek. The farmer told me he had put a native boy up, but the animal had bucked so much no boy would ride it.

The upshot was I should go over next day to try it. Accordingly, I started out for the farm and, as I approached the buildings, met a small boy leading a big roan. I had been told my promised steed was big and grey, and having found people there were vague about colours, I took it that this was the animal. I dismounted from the pony I was hacking over, handed her to the umfaan, transferred the saddle, took the roan from the now gaping boy, and telling him to take my pony to the farm, mounted and set forth.

A collection of natives turned up, all looking amazed, but I imagined that to be due merely to the reputation this horse had earned. However I was a little surprised that my mount was so definitely sleepy, so I turned and rode back to the farm; only to find I had wrested a native boy's horse from the hands of the umfaan he had sent to fetch it, and, "this was not the Lady Clare." The matter was put right, I restored the roan horse and its owner roared and chuckled with delighted amusement when I explained.

Then the farmer's boys brought out the true grey, and the whole family assembled to see the fun, backed up by every African on the place as far as I could see. They all stood well back, told each other to keep away from his heels, and informed me it was my own responsibility, all of which was sufficiently intimidating to add considerably to the accustomed thumping of apprehension inside me. Suppressing the qualms as well as I could, I saddled him up, talked to him a few minutes, pulled his ears, and – mounted. He stood like a rock, we walked quietly down the lane and left the whole gathering like a pricked balloon, disappointed of their expected display.

He was a grand big fellow, nervous and a bit apt to shy, but had no vice whatever. He gave me a lovely ride. I took him off to a peaceful place, got off and had a chat remembering Lady J, and he carried me daily all the rest of the time I was there, as they made me free to go and catch him whenever I would.

I often wondered about his owner, for the grey had a beautiful snaffle bridle of light English leather, most unusual in that country where they appear to lack some tanning secret, South African-made saddlery being stiff, heavy and of poor quality; he had arrived without a saddle, the farmer had gathered that the man had sold it to pay his way. What was his history? How had he come by such a fine horse, for he was infinitely superior to the average mount. Whatever he was, he must have been a horse lover, for that grey knew what it was to have a right understanding and true companionship with his rider. Probably he realised that was lacking when the native got on, and decided to take a firm line from the start.

I found that he had the remains of shoes embedded in four months growth of hoof, so had those off straight away and gradually trimmed the hoof into shape. After riding for time on the turf only, his feet hardened up sufficiently to take us anywhere. The shoes themselves were an indication they had come from far, for horses are not usually shod in those parts; only a very long trek on the roads, or constant roadwork as done by trap-horses necessitates shoeing as a rule, except in cases of extra brittle hooves.

This grey took me on one especially exciting expedition. There is a fine mountain that towers above Kokstad to a height of 7,267 feet. Kokstad itself being about 4,900 feet, there was about 2,300 feet to climb. It is the highest peak in the whole district and promised a glorious view, so I thought the grey and I might see what we could do about climbing it together. The daughter of a retired Basutoland Government official in the neighbourhood also wished to make the ascent of Mt. Currie. She had one of the best real Basuto ponies I ever saw, brought with them from that country. He rejoiced in the name Sincipatu, and was as clever as a cat on steep slopes and among rocks, being well used to such going in his native land. I had no knowledge of my grey's proficiency or otherwise in such places, but I knew something of his heart and did not doubt that we should get there somehow.

The first part of the ride was through attractive country, skirting the base of the mountain and threading through the sites of abandoned small-holdings, a tumbledown mud building here and there, now inhabited by Africans, but hinting at Griqua or European occupation by its shape. Small groups of fruit trees, much overgrown, showed where orchards had been planted near the homesteads. Possibly being situated not far from the township, poor whites had sought to improve their living a little on these small patches of land, but for one reason or another, had had to leave; now they had been absorbed into the farms around, and the old homesteads had become extra dwellings for the natives.

We were soon clear of the accompanying cultivated strips and out on the veld, the grass was long, and there were often hidden boulders, and frequently mountain streams in the creases of the hillside to be negotiated. I did not ride with as loose a rein or unwary an eye as Sincipatu's rider felt justified in doing, but my fellow never let me down, and as we started to climb, threading our way through rocks and odd scrubby bushes, he dug his toes in and fairly threw himself at it.

It was a terrific climb, seeming almost perpendicular for the last few hundred yards. It was all I could do to sit dead still as far forward as possible, keeping my weight clear to free his great thrusting loins for the final effort, when all the time gravity suggested slipping over his tail. With a last tremendous heave, we were up on the neck between the two rocky peaks of the summit, and thankful to take a breather. The good grey had given of his best all the way and he was fairly well done. I off-saddled at once and massaged his sweating back, dried his ears, and then left him to graze gratefully on the narrow neck, knee-haltering him, feeling perfectly confident he would be as sensible about that as about everything else, though again, I had no notion whether he had experienced it before.

We climbed the last few yards with our own hands and feet, and found ourselves on the roof of the world, with a clear cool spring gushing out at the very top in an amazing way. It was glorious to drink at the spring, knowing it to be dead safe, being the source itself. In that country, it is never safe to drink unless close to the source of a spring, as there are so many hazards of contamination on its course, where dysentery and other diseases are rife among the Africans.

Sitting on the one peak of Mt. Currie, we looked across the neck, where our horses grazed peacefully, to the other height, and as we watched, a family of baboons came out and chattered angrily at us. Indeed, their chattering grew into very definite curses, and mothers swore over their babies' heads. An old dog baboon hurled pebbles and imprecations across the space between us, but both fell harmlessly. I hope they relieved his feelings.

When we had gazed long enough on the lovely expanse of East Griqualand laid out on all sides, and eaten our sandwiches in perfect content, we climbed down to saddle up our mounts, now rested and eager to turn for home. We slid down the first few hundred yards, even without our weights, our horses almost grazed their hocks, so sheer was the drop; but they carried us on down incredibly steep places, and showed again how amazingly sure-footed they were. It was wonderful relief to get onto a wattle-shaded path at the base and water our horses at a cool stream, protected from the glare which had scorched us on the descent.

CHAPTER 11

Experience on other farms. Start on own. Fumigation; plumbing

During this time spent care-taking, we saw homes of very varying types, some entirely primitive without light, tap, bath or sink, others with electric light, bathrooms and refrigerators. All had had to battle without any convenience to start with; it was wonderfully encouraging to see the delightful homes people had made. We realised what a satisfying pleasure it must be to look round on the results of one's own efforts as evidenced in each newly acquired comfort.

Eventually, we came to our own farm, GOLDEN FLEECE by name, and started on that stupendous task, when so much needed doing in so many different directions at the same time, that the chief essential was to keep a balanced mind and put first things first with masterly organisation. Accordingly, farm needs came a long way before house, for we came onto the farm in October, which is springtime, and the start of the yearly race from seedtime to harvest, growing time to frost.

We were lucky to have stayed in primitive farmhouses and already learnt to do without many of the things that are taken for granted in the normal household. One can of cold water outside the back door is certainly nearer luxury than a stream two or three hundred yards away; so having lived with that amenity for some months, we were able to feel it luxury indeed to run a pipe through a wall and actually own one tap within. Paraffin tins holding four gallons make admirable containers that stand on a stove all day and hold water perpetually heating, and constantly replenished from that tap deluxe.

Thinking of domestic conditions, quite naturally I find myself talking of water, for certainly that is the first consideration, and much can be endured if this one essential is readily to hand. There was a farmer's wife in the district who had come out from England, and remained very English in her outlook; she had found things most primitive on her arrival, mud floors in the house and no water. After twelve years waiting, her longed-for bathroom had four walls, but was still floorless and bathless. She would take visitors pathetically to see her castle, so much of it still in the air. I am afraid that bathroom procrastinated just too long, for after another few years, she persuaded her husband to retire, and they found refuse in an hotel, where perhaps the number of bathrooms appealed in contrast.

We managed for a couple of years with a tin tub and the aforesaid paraffin tin, but after that, it seemed legitimate to allow ourselves the luxury of a real bath. Having acquired a noble porcelain specimen at a greatly reduced price owing to some quite unnoticeable damage to the rim, it was no time before a 44 gallon petrol drum was set up outside the bathroom wall, and a small brick erection built round it, with fire bars below and a chimney above. Then, sticking a pipe from the drum through that long-suffering wall, it only remained to fill the drum from a feed pipe, light a fire of mealie cobs and malonga (sun-dried cow dung), and there was a hot water supply fit for a king. As cold water did not flow in until a tap was turned on, there was little or no cooling off, the water remained boiling hot inside the drum, and a succession of hot baths was assured. We had taken the precaution of setting the outlet pipe a few inches above the bottom of the drum to obviate boiling dry, and the early demise of our splendid structure. It was the simplest, most effective hot water system imaginable.

However, my recollections of the simple plumbing involved hold painful memories of contortions in a desperately cramped space lying under the bath, fixing the joint of the waste pipe, which would leak out all over the floor instead of discharging its contents outside the wall. It yielded in the end to my own far from fair hands and consented to do its job with the aid of a little red lead and some packing on the thread – triumph – for months, even years I luxuriated in that bath as in no other, savouring the delight of achievement as much as the comfort of a real soak, such bliss after the canary splashings in a tin tub.

While we struggled on the farm to get the land contoured, ploughed and harrowed, fertilized and planted, the cowshed patched and partitioned, workshops stocked, fences mended, sheep dosed, implements tinkered, the house girls got busy with buckets of whitewash following simple fumigation by means of sulphur fumes. Some weeks before moving in, we pasted up cracks round door and window frames, stuffed up the chimneys with sacks, and set alight to a little heap of sulphur in each room, laying a fuse of a length of twine soaked in paraffin, well buried in a heap, and end protruding to ignite. This procedure twice repeated after three weeks' interval was calculated to polish off any unwanted inhabitants. It was certain cheap, easy and effective.

The construction of cupboards from packing-cases was one of the few gestures to comfort in those early days; but we lived well enough, and the cottage was transformed into a pleasant dwelling, reminiscent of those whitewashed Irish cabins, so good to remember.

CHAPTER 12

Widows' help. Loyalty of native labour.

In these first days on our own farm, we had wonderful help from a small bunch of widows. Somehow, during our wanderings in the search for a place to settle, these women had attached themselves, and asked to be allowed to come with us. The first two, we were more than thankful to engage. Over the third, we hesitated, feeling perhaps we should not aspire to more house servants; wondering where we might house so many, for each farm boy must have his own hut for wife and family. Where, then, should we fit in these unattached women?

However, this third widow was a delightful character, the black equivalent of the real old kindly, comfortable nanny of England, a true gentlewoman; she so begged us to take her, that we stretched a point and said she could come, deciding to find outside jobs for some of them, if our indoor staff seemed unnecessarily large.

When, therefore, yet another widow arrived and besought us to give her work, we attempted to be firm and strong-minded, and decline her offer of service. We had ample labour in the house, we had no right to take on more women, who would require housing and feeding, and had no male counterparts to do their share on the farm. We were very definite. No, there was no work for her. Eventually, she was persuaded to depart, and we put her out of mind as we thought; but we were soon to find that she had other intentions.

With amazing persistence, she determined to keep herself firmly in our minds. Whenever we left the farm, there she was, sitting by the roadside, waving to us. With uncanny timing she would appear at the very moment a gate needed opening: her policy of peaceful penetration gained her the victory in the end. There came a day when we just gave up, feeling she meant to work for us, and work for us she did.

She was told that if she came, she must be prepared to do the fowls, and the garden, and the pigs. She accepted joyfully, and ran them all for many years, eventually handing over these tasks to her own granddaughter only when her legs would no longer carry her.

We were to find the widows invaluable, for there were no husbands to cause dissent. So often with a couple, one may be excellent and the other unsatisfactory, or a good worker may have to be lost owing to the misbehaviour of his or her partner. Young girls in the house are always shifting as, invariably, they get married early on. In every way there was much to be said for our little band, they proved their worth for many years; nothing but ill-health ever removed any of them, and when eventually one of them became past work altogether, there was yet another ready to take her place.

These country Africans are primitive people and come to work on the farms direct from their kraals in the native locations, clad in little but the red ochre blanket, which is their accustomed wear. Contact with Europeans puts them into cast-off European clothing, alas! They very soon lose the picturesque appearance with which they leave the kraal.

The influence from Johannesburg and the mines, where in due course at least some member of every family is sure to find his way, seeps in among these simple people, tainting their natural character, colouring their thoughts as well as their clothing. But country life is still their natural way, and over and over again, a youth goes off, attracted by the high pay of the mines, only to return to the farms after a year or two, thankful to get back to his familiar background, and accept a greatly reduced scale of wages.

On the farm he has his own hut and all his family with him, usually with a mother-in-law, sister, and innumerable offspring, almost impossible to place accurately in the family set-up. His work is with soil and stock, he sits in the sun, his back against the hut wall at midday, he drops back into the pace of the ox, with little ambition or thought for the future, "sufficient unto the day."

It is rare to see native handwork in these parts; very simple rush mats, brooms (a mere handful of grasses bound together), and crude black earthenware pots are brought round from time to time, but the craft is by no means general. It is surprising how few can even thatch their own huts, it is unusual to find a real thatcher among the farm boys, someone often has to be summoned from outside the regular boys when there are thatching jobs to be done.

Spinning, dyeing, weaving, carpentry, etc., are taught at mission schools, but the crafts had not, in the time of which I write, really taken hold. The Africans too often leave it all behind when they depart; they tend to the easy way of life, letting things be, making as little effort as need be. It is the more amazing that they can take so much trouble to carry out our wishes, often so strange and incomprehensible to them.

So much that we do or demand must seem odd and unnecessary, queer whims with no possible explanation in their minds. When they first come into the house to work, if they have never seen the white man's domestic ways before, they show plainly how little they understand such extraordinary habits. In one house, a raw native girl in the kitchen, having had no definite order as to what she should prepare for breakfast, felt she must get ahead or nothing would be ready when her mistress should wake; with the remembrance of lunch the day before, she went out into the garden and brought in some of every kind of vegetable she could see. These she cooked, and finding half a jelly in the larder, placed it carefully in the oven, and went to call the mistress for a royal repast.

Failing utterly to see any reason in our extraordinary fancy for sheets as well as blankets on a bed, they will carefully make it up with alternate layers, blanket, sheet, blanket, sheet; I remember many occasions of hilarity over strange notions of table laying.

How very understandable it is that they should find it hard to comprehend our customs, living as they do all together, a family to a hut, sleeping on the floor with a blanket to cover and perhaps an old skin underneath; squatting round the cooking pot, each taking a handful of putu (dry mealie porridge) in turn, passing a tin from hand to hand to quench their thirst. There are no words in their language for chairs, tables, all the apparatus of our complicated scheme of living, which is quite outside their own accustomed ways. However, little by little, they are adjusting the old to the new, and a woman who had worked long in the house begins to covet the comfort of a real bed for herself: more than once I have been commissioned to buy an iron bedstead at a farm sale for a native. Again, they take pride in the erection of a small shelf in their huts, on which they display an enamel cup and plate, perhaps emulating the kitchen dresser.

However slow or lacking in comprehension they may be, I have the greatest regard for them as a whole. Their loyalty and willing service, given with genuine delight, was a joy all through the years; it never wavered, and they became so much part of the family that our interests were very truly theirs. The real distress when our children had to return to school every term was amazing, especially as their departure lightened the work very considerably. Their return for the holidays was greeted with singing and rejoicing; and the more friends they brought, the more work they gave, the better were the natives pleased. Wonderful, generous, splendid people they are.

CHAPTER 13

Character of farm workers

Journeying out to South Africa as a prospective settler in 1937, ignorant of the country and its peoples, I gathered much gratuitous information from fellow travellers. On the whole, I received a misleading account of the Africans: the impression conveyed being of a dirty, dishonest, lazy, unreliable people. All these adjectives may be applied to them, but unfortunately, they might also apply to many white people. The town native may deserve such epithets, but it was my good fortune to deal only with the Bantu of the country, the farm workers. It is my experience that the African is, or can be, what you expect and help him to be: with much simple, natural, inborn nobility added.

Going from farm to farm, it becomes apparent that the character of the majority of the natives on each individual holding conforms to a certain standard that is consistent with the feeling on that particular farm; and although the boys change continually with the constant ebb and flow from the locations and the mines, yet the type remains unchanged from year to year. There are farms where the boys are always "bad", not evil, but just unreliable, unsatisfactory, no pleasure to guide or control. There are other farms where there is an intangible link between master and servant, where there is sympathy and affection, a genuine desire to serve; and the feeling, nebulous and unformed, conveys itself somehow among the huts so that always there is a "good" atmosphere.

Many settlers make the mistake of expecting too much, and never get over their disillusionment, it constantly riles and annoys, and they are in no position to make the most of the material to hand. For these natives are primitive people, they do not comprehend the many strange ways of the European easily, they have different standards of honesty. It is only sense to take a little extra sugar or milk to enhance that surely very dull mealie putu, or a little tea where it would not be missed, and would make such a comforting extra on their lives, that have so little to add zest or cheer; yet I have never found a country African who is not entirely trustworthy over money. They will restore most carefully any coin, from the smallest, least likely to be missed, to the greatest, with equal care, should any be left about or discovered during cleaning operations.

I have never doubted their impeccable honesty in these matters; at the same time, knowing it to be unfair to expose anyone to needless temptation, the principle is the same for black or white. If the boy has the proper loyalty for his master, and the degree of loyalty reflects more on the master than the servant, then that native will guard all his master's possessions with jealous zeal.

For years, I lived alone on that farm, during the term times when my children were away at boarding schools, yet, although it was well known that I was a white woman alone, no other European within a distance of 1½ to 2 miles, never once did I feel it necessary to lock a door. Had any unreliable native chanced to come through the farm, possibly on his way back to the locations after a period working on the mines in the demoralising city surroundings, my own boys would have seen to my safety, I felt sure.

So much for honesty and reliability, there are other ways in which the European can expect too much of the African; one is in comprehension, and another is speed, action. Too many, perhaps the retired army or naval man errs most often in this respect, expect the boy to jump at their orders and act on their commands with precision and despatch; without beginning to realise, first, that in all probability the boy has only dimly understood the order, if at all, because the boss has made little attempt to learn his language; and secondly, that the pace of the ox is the pace of the native, the pace that has belonged to him through the years, and is as much part of him as he is part of the country.

After all, it is his country, we do well to remember this. I think many of us go wrong in our arrogant assumption that we are lords and masters in this country, where it is to me a humbling thought that the African in his generous nobility gives such loyal service to the white man, who has stepped in and taken his land. There is room for us both, but only if we see that the black man has his rightful share, and if we use our progress aright (bedraggled word though it be) to help him towards advantages that can improve his position, make happier his lot. That lot has fallen to him in a fair ground indeed, and to us too who share it with him; but by mishandling, misunderstanding, misjudgement, misuse, much misery has resulted; and that goodly heritage may well turn out to be neither goodly nor an heritage for us in whom lies the major fault.

There is talk everywhere of the growing insolence of the African, and the feeling in the towns is very different from that among the simple country people. The white man has brought progress, he has given many advantages to the black, which cannot be denied; but with the good, much evil has come hand in hand. The old tribal system is in process of destruction, a gradual inevitable result from the impact with our own civilization. Although that system was bound up with savagery, witchcraft and superstition, yet it was a moral system. Losing his own simple traditions of order and convention, the native is left rudderless, adrift. How can we help him steer aright? There is no easy solution to this tremendous problem. Charity in its fullest sense, respect and sympathy are the keys.

We have no right to deny the African education, progress; it is sad that, as always through history, the price is high, and often bitter the rewards. Yet, there is still pleasure in the thought of the essential, inherent goodness in so many I have known; and wonderful satisfaction and content to be found in life alongside them on the farms.

CHAPTER 14

Illumination in sounds and pictures. Burning hillside.

Life on a south African farm seemed to me one of the most varied, exciting, absorbing lives that could be imagined. To the settler at the start of his new life, there is so much to be observed, and a complex study to be made of country, seasons, crops, stock, people, much else.

No two days are alike for a farmer; there are fresh problems to be dealt with every day, however he may plan the work overnight, invariably the morning brings the need for some modification, be it ruled by a change in the weather, the absence of a boy, the sickness of an animal. There is never need to complain of the daily round.

Added to this spice of variety, there is the satisfaction of seeing results, the content that comes to the owner of land as he looks out over his own property and sees visible, tangible proofs of his own industry, concrete development of his own planning and devising: the increase of his flocks and herds, the conservation and enrichment of his soil to the advantage of man and beast. Remembering also the interest of handling animals and humans, and observing their ways; all this combined with the true sense of achievement to be found when almost all daily needs are provided from that land, when living is bound up so completely with the life, it is apparent that a farmer's is probably the most fulfilling of any.

Certainly, without a feeling for soil or stock, or country, it would not appeal, but it is surely from the beginnings of man the natural way of life. In the early chapters of my South African experience there were picturesque details which stand out in my memory as decorations. No story could be dull with such illuminations to grace its pages.

Riding round the farm overseeing the work, countless sounds and pictures enchant. There is poetry in the cry of the ploughboy to his team, that, in harmony with the design of the long strung-out span of nobly striving beasts, plotting across the open expanse of land, backed by the unchanging yet ever varied lie of the mountains, combines in a perfect artistic whole. As he trudges beside his plough, his arms rise and fall in interrupted rhythm to send the long thong of his whip curling out with accurate precision to flick whichever ox should need reminder. With it comes a wonderful stream of sound, picturesque, musical, colourful, a perfect accompaniment to the whole scene – "Malhas, Voltein, Bantus, Villeman, Bles, Roinek, Kleinboy, Vreiman, Blom, Alverd, sebenze abantwan abam, liya litshona lilanga." (Work, my children, for already the sun goes down.) As this exhortation is prefaced by the whole string of names to the team, so, when the boy wishes to turn his span, he calls on the name of the outside leading ox, who bears across at the word, and leads the team round. I have known newcomers, unconversant with the language, not unnaturally confuse the words, imagining the boy to be calling out the equivalent of right and left: possible jottings to that effect in the notebook of the earnest settler intent on learning the language, might find surprising contradictions next day, a different pair being in the lead.

It is a language picturesque not only in the colourful phrasing, but also in the sound of the words; many are onomatopoeic, and the native delights to emphasise this quality, lengthening and lingering on certain syllables to stress the significant sound. How perfectly *uçingo* expresses the ping of a taut stretched strand of wire, the middle syllable in this case drawn out sometimes to incredible lengths. *Duduma*, the vowels sounded appropriately, conveys the rumble of distant thunder without question.

The African is extremely observant, as is to be expected of those whose natural life is dependent on the land and the vagaries of nature; when every bird, insect, or leaf may tell a tale of events, or foretell things to come. Their weather lore is profound, and they possess knowledge of potent herbs, handed down from father to son, much interwoven with superstition, but holding a core of real value. Their acute observation of any slight peculiarity or special characteristic in people leads to the bestowal of a native name on every European; this name invariably reflecting, often with genius, some very individual trait in the recipient. They will not always disclose the name, particularity if it might be considered uncomplimentary. Sometimes, if asked to explain the meaning of a name that has been heard but not understood, they will prevaricate, try to avoid a direct answer, or even give a wrong interpretation to evade disclosing the true significance.

It may be an unusual nose, a slight tilt to the head, unnoticed by the casual observer, a distinctive laugh, a habit of manner, a subtle likeness to some animal or the markings of a bird, or again, some individual custom or propensity that gives inspiration to the native name. It is always fascinating to discover the names of one's neighbours, and often revealing.

There need be little craving for the entertainments provided for city dwellers, when such variety performances are in constant production, an integral part of this full life. Many colourful details of the farming round claimed interest and appreciation in those early days. As I strove to understand a very little of all that went on among the natives, and adjust previous standards to the ways of the country, the seasons came and went, bringing such a wealth of new events and experiences, it was impossible to assess and sort them all. Little by little over a period of years, the canvas extended, and more and more detail has been filled in. It is a picture that does not pall, and there is no limit to its appeal.

One of the first highlights that stands out in my memory is the sight of a neighbour burning his hillside. Looking out at dusk, I saw a line of fire on the hill across the stream, startling in the half-light, brilliant, exciting, as darkness fell with that swiftness that still surprised me there.

The thin streak of fire crept slowly up and up the hill at first, as though a stream of liquid fire defied the laws of gravity and seeped gradually upward. As I watched, another trickle started downward from the summit, flowing down at the same pace to unite with the stream that climbed to meet it. They joined, and the whole snakelike wearing line from top to bottom of the hill now edged swaying across, making little progress against the wind, which conjured it to send up crests of flame here and there through its sinuous length.

Suddenly from the far side of the hill, a great fiery serpent leapt across, its length stretched like the other from summit to base; but where that first snake oozed and crept, this looped and straightened with the urgency of the wind behind it, sending up great tongues of flame, and lessening the gap between the two glowing reptiles at an incredible speed. The dark sky was luminous with the glow from this fire as it devoured the whole hillside. Then the two lines met, joined in one final up-rearing crest of brilliant flame, to be repeated all up and down the hillside as loop touched loop, and with that last fling, the flames faltered and fell, leapt again, and one by one died, till the hill was once more in darkness, save for a flash, a gleam here and there where a smouldering heap of malonga was fanned again to a flicker and then expired.

It was a wonderful sight in the deep of the South African night, and was to become very familiar during the months of August and September. The fiery snakes crept across much of the surrounding veld when the spring rains were judged to be safely near, or after the first rain had fallen, for in those days, burning off the rank grass was very general. In later years, it became less frequent a custom, for there is no doubt the constant burning weakens the roots of the grass. It used to be considered the only method to clear the rank growth of sour grass that grows out during the summer rains, and being unpalatable to the stock, is left ungrazed. When this coarse tangle is cleared by burning, the young green of the spring growth comes through as soon as there is sufficient moisture to bring it on, and is readily available for the stock. Apart from the damage done to the roots by successive scorchings, tufts of sweet grass tend to remain protected among patches of the sour, and are spared to go to seed. Thus saved from the severity of the frosts at that altitude, 5,000 feet, if not destroyed by burning, these tufts disperse their seeds, and the good grass gets an extra hold on the veld.

Where growth is so rank, it is inadvisable to leave it; by mowing, the sour grass itself can be turned to good use as compost. The mown grass may be manured and trodden into a valuable fertilizing agent in the cattle kraal, and the roots of the sweet grass are left undamaged. Of course, it is not practicable to mow on steep hillsides, or among rocks, so there is always some necessity to burn, though often it could be left out with advantage. If it has to be done, it is better to burn immediately after a rain, when sufficient moisture holds in the base of the tufts to prevent the scorching. The dry top growth is burnt off without destroying the roots.

Picturesque as the burning can be from a distance, it is one of the most arduous and anxious of all farm jobs. As a preliminary some weeks before burning is definitely contemplated, fire-lines are ploughed. A couple of furrows are turned, the one against the other, all down the length of the boundaries. This creates a fair width of inverted sods, the long tinder like dry grasses safely underneath, a sufficient break to make it possible to beat out flames that have had no chance to get their heads. Accordingly, a second line of two furrows width is ploughed parallel about three yards from the first, then, in the late evening, or occasionally early morning, when winds are less liable to blow suddenly gusty or change their quarter without warning, these strips of grass between the two boundary lines are burnt off to form a really wide break.

Such a stretch of bare ground is calculated to stop most grass fires, though there are anxious times when a sudden gust of terrific velocity can cause the flames to jump an incredible width, or a whirlwind can carry tufts of flaming grass or smouldering malonga at a speed that no firebreak can withstand. Thus, the operation is always tricky, and it is impossible to leave any fire without watchers on the windward boundary until every tuft and heap of malonga is surely extinguished. Neighbours combine together, calling out every available boy on both farms to burn these precautionary "breaks". A strong posse of boys, each armed with a wet sack, stands by on each side of the strip, a lighter with a mealie cob on the end of a strong wire and a tin of paraffin, into which he dips his cob from time to time, puts in the fire by touching off tufts with his flaming cob all down the inside of each furrow. The lighter on the downwind furrow goes ahead to allow the flames to eat back against the wind a yard or so before the fire put in behind him from the parallel furrow can tear across and gather too much momentum. By this means, an occasional flick with a wet sack at some obstinate tuft keeps the whole operation in control, and the strip is steadily burnt off all down the boundary.

It is the unexpected that demands every precaution and the extra man-power. A chancy gust from the wrong quarter, or a mischievous dust-devil (whirlwind) can set off a flame beyond the furrow, then it is gruelling work for every possible pair of hands, and the scotch-cart loaded with milk-cans of water that follows along the line, is a wonderful relief to the anxious organizer. When sacks have become charred and start flaming themselves, only spreading the fire they seek to quench, a water supply on the spot is the only hope. With miles of bone dry grass ahead, a tongue of flame on the wrong side of a firebreak is patently terrifying. The relentless power of fire in these moments, when it is touch and go whether man can prevail, calls out primitive fear of the elements: that power if not checked by ingenuity, can become superhuman in a matter of minutes. Should the runaway really get its head, the only solution is to rush all the manpower far enough ahead to put in another break before the flames. But the wind can carry at such speed, only by use of cars or lorries can such a manoeuvre work in time. Half a dozen farms, their stacks, and even huts as well, can be burnt out too easily.

Firebreaks on all boundaries safely burnt, the actual burning of a camp is a comparatively simple matter. As before, the fire is put in on the downwind boundary so that it can start licking back against the wind, steadily widening the burnt area, and making it less and less likely that any wind should cause the main fire to break bounds. This done, it is touched off all down the upwind side, and allowed to have its head. A few watchers, wet sacks in hand, see that all is safe, till the last smouldering ember dies out, and nothing remains in the darkness save that pungent smell of new charred vegetation to tell of the evening's labour, with all its hazards.

One night, long after the burn had apparently died out, I saw a sudden great flame in the darkness. It was well in the middle of the burnt area, so would do no harm. However, I went out to investigate, and found an old hollow dead willow tree on fire. To be on the safe side, I bailed buckets of water from a stream for about half an hour with only my Great Dane's assistance. The result next day, a lot of quite fine charcoal, which I collected for my charcoal cooling safe (my only kind of refrigeration). Water trickling continuously over the charcoal, packed between double sides of wire netting, the evaporation producing the cooling agent. Simple and effective.

Beautiful indeed is the night of the burning, but morning brings a dreary sight of scorched and blackened veld, unbelievable that such can be a promise of spring.

CHAPTER 15

Seasons. Oxen.

One of the first essentials for the settler in a new country is to adjust to the different seasons, to learn the pattern of cultivation, of seed-time and harvest.

Landing in South Africa for the first time in early April, which is autumn, the last rains of the summer had come just before my arrival, and I was to be in the country for five months before I saw a single drop of rain. Even then, it meant no break in the winter drought, as I should have known all too well from all the signs, had I then the experience of later years.

Eventually, after a week of hot weather, it suddenly turned cold, clouds came up, and there were a few scanty showers of sleet. The thrill of hearing those few raindrops on the iron roof after all those months was indescribable, and I rushed out to savour the glorious smell of wet earth at last. Next morning we woke to a white and lovely world, but the sky was clear again, the sun came out in all his strength, and in an hour or two, no trace of snow or even moisture could be seen. The distant mountains showed their snow-caps, but on the nearer range, it melted almost as we watched.

That small scurry was insufficient to make any impression on the parched earth, and it was to be another two months before rain came in earnest. We became accustomed to watching the promise come and go, gradually nearer and nearer, only to disappoint again and again. Such is the way of things in that climate, and it is normal to have no rain from April to September, October, or even later in bad seasons. Dry winters are the rule, the farmer's constant struggle is to grow enough feed during the few months of summer rains and to ripen it before the frosts of April come to kill the crops that have not been harvested in time.

All through those dry winter months the stock must depend on feed grown for them through the summer: hay, roots, ensilage, grain, and such green feed as oats and wheat, sufficiently frost resisting to yield a little grazing. For the fierce frosts of the high veld kill all the goodness in the natural grass. The only animals to subsist on the veld alone have a very meagre time of it indeed, and emerge weak, bony and listless at the end of the winter.

Native cattle and ponies all too often have to keep themselves alive on this unsatisfying fare, but the patient farm ox too somehow contrives to live through till the spring rains are judged to be sufficiently near to warrant the allowance of a ration of second-rate hay, too poor for the pampered cows, or an old straw stack that would rot if left through the summer rains.

Such is the fare meted out to the ox, the most economic proposition on the whole farm, in the time of which I write. Now, alas, tractors have almost entirely taken their place on European farms, time-saving and practical though they are, undoubtedly, I should miss the ox sorely, were I to return to that life, now, sadly, more than unlikely.

The old ox did most of the work on the farm, lived only on such feed as could be spared from the cossetted cows and sheep, put back into the soil in manure more in value than ever it fell to his lot to get out of it, and at the end of a useful life of hard toil, he was sold for twice the sum that was paid for him, if things went as they should. If his teeth were watched carefully, and he was thrown out of work before he got too old to fatten, he got a last season of good feed and no work, thus commanding a good price at the abattoir.

I often wondered what surprise he must have felt when he reached that final season and found himself free from the shoots and blows, and the heavy yoke that were his normal lot; and with what amazement he must have viewed the succulent feed to which he was introduced for the first time in his life. Feed that hitherto he had only snatched surreptitiously on illicit excursions resulting from some unlatched gate. Or had he ceased to wonder? Was he content in his traditional patience to accept whatever came to him, unquestioning?

I like to think this last taste of freedom and good fare made up a little for the lean years, but it was small compensation for his life of service.

He is a grand fellow. I had a great regard for him at all times. Like all animals, they have their individual characteristics, and there can be real rogues, skellums as they are called, who never give in but battle for their independence to the end. Although there may be a struggle with a young ox when training him to the yoke, he usually gives in eventually, and it is always the ox that gave the most trouble in training, who becomes the best worker. The energy he put into his resistance goes into his work, and these are the oxen chosen by the boys to lead in the span, for they set the standard for the whole team.

The African, who is so fond of children and, practically without exception, invariably good to them, can be astonishingly cruel to animals. When an ox lies down in the yoke, it is sometimes necessary to use harsh words and methods to get him up; but the natives have to be watched, or they will go too far, and often permanently injure the animal.

Hot irons are sometimes used, and it is extraordinary what a determined ox will stand without giving in. I have seen smoke rising with the sickly smell of burnt hair and skin while the ox lies immovable, an occasional rumbling, suppressed bellow of pain the only indication of his discomfort. The native will allow the hot irons to sear right into the flesh, and actually destroy the tissues unless one intervenes. It may be permissible to use the point of an iron as a goad, frequently the animal will take the hint and jump to it, and be no further trouble; but the prolonged torture is very wrong indeed. I have seen oxen with open sores from such treatment that refuse to heal. Again, sometimes the boys will twist the tail till the joint is actually broken, when eventually the end drops off and the quarters are left cruelly exposed to the flies.

It sometimes works to inspan a full team, including the conscientious objector, and when he lies down, take no notice of his passive resistance, but set the team in motion and have him dragged a few steps; but unless a sharp eye is kept on the proceedings, the boys will allow him to be dragged over rough ground till he is seriously injured, even sometimes dragged to death.

On every farm there were two or four oxen, impossible to confuse with the main bunch, the milk-cart team. Assured, complacent, placidly confident in their position, they stroll calm and unhurried from the yoke when outspanned, in sharp contrast to the usual working ox, who jerks away the moment the yoke is lifted, with such an evasive twist that his horn may easily catch the unwary native or rip his blanket. Poor fellow, he has so little in his life, he must snatch all he can get: the first out of the yoke may find and extra mouthful, steal an illicit bite of green feed or slice of turnip from the cows, before he is chased off to his own dull grazing. Not so the milk-cart ox, he knows himself to be a trusted old retainer. To be on hand for the early morning carting to the cheese factory, these few oxen sleep in some nearby paddock, where perforce they must have their quota of feed put out for them. Thus with the minimum of effort these aristocrats sustain themselves with far more satisfying fare than that of their plebeian brethren, who must roam far over a large expanse of veld to wrest what nourishment they can from the inhospitable pasture.

The comfortable situation of these favoured animals is immediately obvious in their general demeanour: it was amusing to find them at noon contentedly chewing the cud in their own chosen patch of shade, like old gentlemen in their favourite armchairs at the Club.

Becoming acquainted with individual traits among the working oxen of the farm, watching their condition, and overseeing the inspanning at the start of the day, there was constant interest and pleasure to be found. Pride in a well-matched span of these fine beasts can be as great as that in a team of plough horses, which says much.

CHAPTER 16

First horses. Breaking-in

Through all the varied farm doings, horses were never out of things. Those three which came on loan, shortly after our arrival in the country, were two farm hacks of plebeian breeding, a gelding and a mare, the third was a yearling colt still running with his dam, while she was already heavy in foal. The colt came only because no-one had attempted to wean or handle him, so automatically he stayed with the mare. The other two, it was kindly thought, might be useful for the children to ride, as they were quiet reliable hacks. Both children had everything to learn, having had no previous opportunity to ride at all, and Con, the gelding, proved himself to be the ideal beginner's pony. Indeed, he was destined to teach a whole succession of children after my own, as eventually Christmas cheques from grandparents in England chanced to coincide with the later decision of Con's owner to sell him. By that time, his value as a child's pony was well known to us, and it seemed too good an opportunity to miss, the wherewithal so opportunely at hand. The children accordingly purchased him jointly for the modest sum of £11, the odd £1 being contributed on the spot to make up the total. Never has there been a more entirely satisfactory deal. He continued to the age of twenty-eight, and not only taught many beginners, but was the reliable mount for all nervous guests, and always a much loved friend and retainer.

One characteristic he never outgrew. It took all the boys on the farm to round him up and pen him in the corner of a camp, and even then, he could whip round and with a wicked low shake of head charge through the circle and be off. He did not approve at all of surrendering to natives, and it was with the reputation of being well-nigh impossible to catch that he came to us for that first visit. It took a great deal of perseverance indeed, in a small paddock, to teach him to come to me, but I won in the end, and thereafter could be reasonably certain of catching him whenever I wanted him, provided I went alone. But, to the end, if accompanied by anyone else, he could decide to be contrary, in which case there was only one thing to be done – send everyone away, sit on the ground, and show my own complete unconcern – then, the proper atmosphere restored, the matter was simple, although there were occasions when, being in a hurry, I had to cut short the calming preliminaries, and the only method of securing him was to lift a foreleg surreptitiously, while talking to him, apparently quite uninterested in his head. Let a native attempt to help, and the game was up.

He was a wily old man and a character from the start, but no pony could have been more wonderful in the care he took of those children. He could be relied on to carry them at all paces, perfectly safely, and his canter was so smooth it hardly lifted them in the saddle, so they quickly acquired confidence. He was no slug, so there was never any of that maddening kicking with no response that is so defeating for the young rider, and that can teach such bad habits, difficult to unlearn.

In this connection, I have a picture in my mind of my own small son aged only three, his legs as yet so short they failed to reach beyond the saddle flaps, with little idea of how to convey his wishes to Con, who stood patiently waiting for some recognisable order to proceed. He tried for a time to induce momentum by swaying his body back and forth, much as he increased his speed on his tricycle, then, finding this method quite unavailing, he called out to the diminutive Intombazan standing by, "Pus me, Linnan". Another recollection of the same combination at that time is of a pause in Con's progression while he delicately scratched an ear with a contortionate hind hoof. His small rider perched securely on top, with an expression of surprise at such a gymnastic display that rivalled Con's attitude in provoking mirth from the onlookers.

Mary, the roan mare, did her best too, and as the children's riding was not very exacting in those early days, she was able to carry on until the time of foaling. Meanwhile, I was having a lot of fun trying out the methods described in Calthrop's book, "The horse as Comrade and Friend," which I had often longed to put to the test.

Mary's colt, a roan native-bred fellow, had never been handled, but was quite ready to trust us. It did not take long to teach him to lead, and he seemed to enjoy the sessions when I could find time to halter him, handle him all over, and do a lot of talking. Before long, I put aside a longer afternoon, collected a short strap and a longer rope, took him into a smallish ploughed land, in default of the recommended straw yard, and got busy.

He knew my voice, so it was no difficulty to strap up the near foreleg, and encourage him to tire himself out in the heavy plough on three legs. He could not see any point in this, not unnaturally, and would keep coming back to me to suggest I might release him from the discomfort, poor fellow. Eventually, when he showed signs of exhaustion, it was a comparatively simple matter to pull his head round to the off by means of the rope passed over his withers, and with a final plunge or two, he was down. I was at his head at once, but there was no fight in him, and he lay flat out, giving me the opportunity to handle him everywhere, even to his tongue. Before he had recovered fully from the physical exhaustion, he began to take an interest in my voice, and found the hand rubbing definitely pleasant. I unstrapped the foreleg and massaged the overflexed joint; soon we had established an excellent understanding, and I then encouraged him to get on his feet once more.

It was good to find no reaction away from me, no resentment of such handling, and the confidence created while he lay on the ground, completely under my control, was to last; his vastly superior physical strength being unable to assert itself, the illusion of my own superiority was conveyed for all time.

A young horse must never be allowed to know his own strength, or the game is lost; this was certainly a rapid method, and followed up by normal handling, produced satisfactory results. I put him down once again a little later, and introduced a bit at the same time; he was not surprised or alarmed at any of the introductions to tack as they came along.

After a perfectly usual course of lungeing, during which he learnt to adjust his pace to the word, stand, rain back, etc., in the normal way, I mounted him without any difficulty whatever; he had felt my weight across him as he lay on the ground, for I had made him lie up on an even keel at the end of the second lesson, got across him and let him feel the pressure of my calves, so it all came to him very easily, and was an interesting experience. Later, this colt became the property of my daughter, his kind owner offering him to her as we had really brought him up. We made it a serious deal by putting on him the price of 2/6, which she was able to pay for herself, just so that she might be able to look him in the mouth at any time!

The colt, Pip, became a sturdy hack up to any amount of weight, but his lack of quality was felt in his paces which were always "rough", he was also too stocky a build and coarse in the wither, so when in a few years' time, I was asked to find a mount for a young schoolmaster, who wished to hire an animal to carry him on a trip through Basutoland, Pip seemed just the sort. He was staunch and untiring, and should do all that would be required of him on such a journey. He was duly hired, and at the end of the trip, his rider asked if he might buy him, as he had become so attached to him. It was an ideal solution, for Pip would be genuinely appreciated, whereas with us, although much loved, he did not really suit his job.

By that time, there were several other mounts in my string and little time for those whose training was complete, as far as it went, for Pip was never the sort to make a polo pony; but he had done his bit, giving me the thrill of the very first ride on an animal handled entirely from the start by myself.

There is nothing to beat it, when the young thing under you responds to your own careful training and you put into practice the lessons of the previous weeks. Everything is new and reactions may be unexpected, but it is pure delight to find your pupil relying on the instructor's steady guidance and finding reassurance in the voice to which he had learnt to listen. Every step of the ride is full of interest, and it is fatal to relax attention for a moment, every faculty must be on the alert, and the pupil must never sense any waver of doubt in the mind of his guide, so it is excellent training too for one's own self-control. I was to experience the thrill many times over, each time, though compounded of the same elements, it was different, for no two horses were ever alike, nor ever will be, but I owe to Pip that first initiation, so he had earned a very definite place in this chronicle.

Next on the scene came Pip's own half-sister, destined to take his place and become my daughter's own pony, which position she held to the end. The roan mare, Mary, foaled down while they were still in my charge. A common mare herself, she was in foal to a local thoroughbred stallion, so her offspring might be expected to show more quality than her half-brother. Here was another new experience, long anticipated, though not to be compared with the birth of the first foal I bred myself from my own mare, yet joy enough to be in on the spot for that foal's arrival.

As it happened, we were away for the night at a neighbour's farm when the foal chose to put in an appearance. On our return, the boys reported that the mare had foaled, but added that no-one had been able to get near her, she was very wild. I was sorry about this, for it sounded as though she had been chased. Mary had gone off with her foal to the top of the farm. Camps are large on South African farms, and may extend over many hundreds of acres, so it was a longish walk to get up to her. The children were, of course, longing to look at the foal, but I had to let them see the small form from a considerable distance, and then exhort them to patience till I should have had time to establish quiet trust with the mare.

I did not know to what extent she might have been alarmed, or how jealous a mother she might prove to be. At sight of people, she retreated yet further, but when I went on alone, she let me come up to her, and although she was apprehensive at first, and took care to get between me and her foal, doing a good deal of blowing, it was not long before I was scratching her neck with one hand and the foal's back with the other. During our absence, boys had probably thrown clods to see the foal gallop, hence her nervous fears, for at all subsequent foalings at which I have been privileged to be first on the scene, the mares have never failed to welcome me, even wanting to show off their foals if maternally minded, or occasionally seeming to be more anxious to talk to me, almost inviting me to commiserate over the nuisance of the impatient new arrival.

Mary's foal proved to be a light bay filly with a star on her forehead, and a most attractive little dish face. She had not much quality to boast, but certainly promised better than her half-brother in this respect. However, on that first day of days, her breeding mattered not a jot, it was pure joy to be handling a foal that showed complete confidence in this, her first human contact. I shall not forget the feel of that small body under my hands, as I experienced for the first time, that recurring marvel, the charm of which did not fade, but was reborn with every foal.

Next day, although the children were warned to keep their distance, they could not resist coming into view, and the mare, seeing other figures in the offing, made off wildly, her foal careering valiantly at her side. The other horses who had joined Mary all seemed very wild, and I now felt sure boys had chased them while we were away. It took me some time to come up with them and dispel their alarm. It was bitter to think the horses were wild after all the time and patience that had gone to taming them, and teaching them to be caught in the open veld. I need not have worried, for the following day, on my going up to the camp alone, Con and the colt both walked straight up to me, and wanted all the attention I could spare them.

Then I moved on to within a few yards of where Mary was grazing, stood still and waited; the colt followed me over, so I sat down and let him nudge me and have a chat. In a few minutes up came Mary and put her nose in for a share of the conversation, at the same time warning Pip to keep clear of her foal. I kept very still, just doing a bit of nose rubbing which she enjoyed; another few minutes and the three day old filly was nuzzling me all over, sticking her nose into my face in under my hat, and wriggling with delight as I scratched her back. Slowly kneeling up beside her, I rubbed her all over, even lifted her feet. She put her long foreleg with its miniature perfect hoof onto my knee, and was delighted to have it lifted and gently shaken. Meanwhile the mare looked on calmly, and seemed to like the attention I gave to her baby. She never warned me once, though the colt was warned off if ever he attempted to nose the foal. Poor chap, he was a little jealous, and kept giving me pushes in the back, and occasionally pawed me, saying plainly, "Do stop playing with that and talk to me." So I rubbed the filly with one hand and the colt with the other, till eventually I had to tear myself away from their perfect company.

The filly grew out in time to a 14.3 fairly stocky mare. She had always a completely trusting nature, never losing that early confidence in people. She was no trouble at all to break in, indeed, much of her training came to her almost naturally. She was so accustomed to the voice, she seemed to understand intuitively what was wanted, and I remember the first time I mounted her, neither she nor I felt a quiver of apprehension, it seemed quite normal to both of us.

There was a little trouble teaching her to stand to be mounted, for she would be impatient to set off, but a few minutes in the confined space of the sheep kraal, penned in a corner for a few days while I mounted and dismounted, teaching her just what "stand" should mean, and that was a lesson learnt for all time.

One more tussle we had, she and I, over reining back: she would dig in her toes and refuse to budge, till one day she went up on end rather than yield, and being on a slope, she came right over backwards. Fortunately, neither of us were hurt, and I was able to press home the advantage, remounting instantly, repeating the aids and the command; she obeyed at once and there was no further trouble.

So complete was the trust and confidence we had in each other, that I could ride her about like an old horse from the start, and she was safe for the children long before a young horse can be trusted as a rule. She also became the property of my children on much the same terms as Pip, and as Rima she remained one of the regular farm hacks, being ridden by any visitor, taking a boy for the post, or any other job that might crop up.

Her build and lack of quality made her unsuited for polo. She also had a ewe neck which prevented her flexing properly, and, though comfortable enough, she was clumsy and lacked the "snap" without which a polo pony makes heavy weather. For all that, she had a very warm place in everyone's affections. How could it be otherwise with such a kindly disposition, and when she had been our very first familiar foal.

Later she took part in a great expedition to the Drakensberg, serving as packhorse, so she will appear again.

CHAPTER 17

Hailstorm devastation

Horses obviously loomed large on the scene, but they were merely a side-line, indulged in for my own delight. The real vital business of farming was of course our chief concern, and in this, as for every farmer the world over, weather was a major factor.

Very early on in our experience, we were subjected to one of the violent hailstorms prevalent in that area. When a hailstorm was approaching from across the Flats which formed part of our farm, there was a strange ominous roar as the storm swept ever nearer, devastating every growth, stripping stems of every leaf, leaving gaunt bare stalks in desolation. The hailstones were often as large as golf-balls, and cattle would suffer sadly, often their hides ruined by the marks left inevitably by these pounding missiles. Sheep, though perhaps more protected by the thickness of their fleeces, were sometimes killed outright when one of these lethal bolts from the sky fell on a head, or found its target a lamb with fleece as yet too spare.

The helplessness of mere humans in the face of this relentless power was akin to that we feel when pitted against other forces of nature, fire, flood, and raging seas. Only supernatural powers might sometimes prevail. I have seen the Africans come out in a body with tins and staves, call out and beat their tins, commanding the storm to spare them, and I have actually witnessed the apparent submission of that storm as it suddenly turned off in an acute angle, and took its path away from the lands where all the crops would have been destroyed.

It was a truly magical sight, uncanny, subliminal, somehow linked to the primitive nature of these country Africans who, ,just as children, retain their touch with the Infinite until civilization and conventional learning comes in to block, or perhaps crowd out that unconscious faculty to tune in to a Power beyond our normal adult recognition.

Our first severe set-back came when just such a storm struck the farm shortly after our first crops were showing excellent promise. We had been bidden to tea with farming friends, some six or so miles away, and as we approached their farm, the storm hit us, the car was put out of action with water in the cylinders, rain poured in through the broken windows. I had to kneel up holding a rug across the worst gaps, until another farmer came up behind and got his bumpers against ours, pushing us to our destination, only five minutes before the bridge leading to the farm was swept away. The dam above had burst with the rush of flood water.

There we were marooned for the night with a useless car, and the house temporarily isolated with rushing torrents sweeping down on each side. Several other tea-guests were also forced to stay the night, our good hosts, as ever in that district, quite unperturbed at the prospect of finding beds for eight extras with no warning. It would have been a pleasant interlude had it not been for our dread of the spectacle we might find when we got back to our own farm eventually.

We were as yet ignorant of the breadth of that particular storm. Those hailstorms are not very wide as a rule but carve a strip right through the lands in their path, and leave unscathed the ground on either side. Alas, when we did reach home next day, it was to discover that we had been right in the path of the hail.

The dam wall on the farm above us had broken, water rushed down and carried away most of our fences, ten in all, as well as thirteen sheep. Only one camp remained stock-proof, all others allowed cattle or sheep to wander where they would. Soil had washed badly in some lands; although contour banks held fairly well, the force of water was too great and swept over the tops. Beside all this, the hail had stripped the mealies, only bare stalks remained standing. The gardens were completely ruined, not a vestige of colour to be seen in the flower garden, sad battered stalks without flower or leaf all that remained. Vegetables appeared non-existent or smashed beyond hope of recovery. Gone were all our winter supplies, and thoughtful relays of planting. Fruit trees were bare of leaf and fruit, the latter on the ground, pitted and bashed. The back rooms of the cottage leaked like sieves, the children's room a sea of mud, a piece of the wall having fallen in.

Where to begin repairs and replanting was a problem with such devastation all around. Fencing took priority, as stock must be confined, and we then had to work out what crops might possibly have time to mature before winter would catch us out. Luckily rebuilding a wall of the cottage could be done in somewhat primitive fashion with sods, quickly plastered and whitewashed in keeping with the main building. Jams and jellies were made with any parts of the fruit that could be salvaged from the ground.

Still on the weather subject, we had a wonderful example of the generous and imaginative neighbourliness of the farming community in our corner of East Griqualand. We were struck by a hurricane which blew topsoil, dried up the land already threatened by drought, and took the corrugated iron, pitched roof clean off the engine shed, buckling it badly in the process. I was posed with a teaser to replace it with my unskilled boys. One of our good neighbours shortly passed by the road through the farm and took a good look at it. That evening, four of our nearby farmers rang up to say, "Expect a gang tomorrow morning." I killed an extra fowl, made more bread in readiness, and they arrived, complete with tools, timber, and spare boys. I had assembled all mine and every available ladder. One of the womenfolk came along with them to help me carve and cut up. We fed them all on the verandah, while the boys joined ours at the huts. By 3.30, the roof was in perfect order once more, with new beams and timbers where necessary.

As always, when meeting that small farm community en masse, I felt renewed gratitude for the kindly providence which allowed us to find our farm amid such neighbours.

CHAPTER 18

Drought

"O, Western wind, when wilt thou blow
That the small rain down can fall?"[3]

From hail and hurricane to drought with a capital D; the worst farming hazard in a way, because instead of sudden disaster which strikes without forewarning, so that you are plunged straight into the battle to repair, replan and revive with little time to bemoan, drought comes on remorselessly, day after day it creeps nearer with grim foreboding. Again, man is helpless against this cruel insidious crime of nature. Day after day, hopes would rise, as most convincing clouds in the right quarter, which normally presage rain, came up on the horizon, but as hopes rose, so did the wind: clouds, rain and hopes all were swept away together.

This incessant wind gradually dried up every remaining vestige of moisture. It really hurt to go out each morning to a yet more arid and barren aspect. One by one, springs, pans, dams, dried up until finally only one spring on the whole farm survived. Milking cows had to drink at a trough filled by the windmill with water from underground, but oxen and sheep kept going while the spring lasted; the latter only brought up on alternate days to drink, as a daily trek would have weakened them too much. Feed was desperately short, as all green stuff withered away. Eventually, we lopped willow branches, greening in early spring, for the cattle to browse their leaves, the only green feed on the farm. Finally, the district was declared a drought-stricken area which allowed cheap rates on the railway, enabling farmers to buy Lucerne or oats from further afield. Milk cans conveying milk to the cheese factory returned daily filled with water from the more plentiful supply there.

---

[3] The first lines of an early 16th Century song taken from a medieval poem

So we existed day by day, ever more anxious, until in a final effort at a solution I went off up to the Berg in search of grazing for hire for the dry stock, judging they could no longer subsist on our arid farm, the last trickles of water had to be meted out to the cows that were in milk. I returned, having arranged to trek the oxen, dry cows and sheep slowly up to the foothills, where springs still ran, for the mountains always catch more rain. I was fearful as the stock were weak after the prolonged shortage; however, it was the last remaining hope.

That night I went to bed full of anxious thoughts, planning the stages the cattle might be expected to travel, deciding to hire a lorry for the weaker sheep, resolved to be up extra early to send them on their way. As I lay there, my mind too full for sleep, what did I hear? Could it be drops of rain on the roof? This was unbelievable after months of promise unfulfilled. The usual clouds had shown on the horizon, but we had long ceased to put any trust in them. It was true, the drops quickened, and soon a glorious steady rain was pounding the tin roof. That rain continued for three days, exactly what we needed, not a violent short-lived downpour that would have run off the parched ground, washing away topsoil, finishing before the moisture could sink in.

This heaven-sent rain seeped into the thirsty soil, gradually springs took heart once more. What joy to cancel the grazing up country, and put away those desperate anxieties for the weakened stock. It is a glorious country despite these terrifying hazards, and can recover incredibly quickly. It seems to turn green overnight, and so it was. Always, I have loved rainy days, they remind me of mountain walks in Ireland with soft rain in one's face all day, and such marvels in colouring. As a farmer, conscious of all it does for the land, with what joy and gratitude we welcome a long steady soaking.

The experience of that terrifying drought prompted me to build (with the help of a local Griqua artisan) a large reservoir, which would collect the water pumped by the windmill whenever winds obliged, and thus circumvent the long windless periods which were wont to occur. Bricks from an ancient store, long since derelict, served well, and a fortunate purchase of piping from the farrier in the local dorp almost saw us through. Stocks and dies to thread the pipes were borrowed from an ever-helpful neighbour, and we were away. When the structure had been lined with an extra strong cement mixture, all that remained was to contrive a thatched roof on stilts, close the gap with wire-netting to defeat any birds intent on an illicit bath, remembering to incorporate a light door allowing easy access for occasional cleaning out. A padlock on this door gave us confidence that no venturesome umfaans might aspire to a dip, and we experienced the comforting thought of plenty of water for house and dairy, come what may. We had built the reservoir on a rise well above our cottage, so our needs were gravity-fed, simple and effective, like much else.

CHAPTER 19

Farm events. Shearing. Sheep dosing and dipping. Dipping cattle.

Remembering the varied seasons and major landmarks of our farming year, sheep shearing stands out. Sometime in October or November (spring) a band of about ten African shearers arrived, their advent heralded a day or two previously by a message from a neighbour to say he had almost finished his shearing, and I could expect the band.

Preparations were made immediately, the stable cleared, and a sorting table set up. This was slatted to allow odd scraps and dust to fall through when fleeces were spread on it. Large mesh wire-netting for a top sometimes sufficed, but this was not so satisfactory. Frames to support the huge bales supplied by the Wool Board were fixed and marked for the different qualities, e.g., 1st, 2nd, Lambs, Pieces, and Locks. A holding area was partitioned off to constrain the sheep within easy reach of the shearers. It was necessary to bring up all the sheep to paddocks nearby, and sort them into groups, so that those carrying wool of a certain type should give a run of similar fleeces, which can go into the same bale. The price obtained for each bale is that due for the worst wool in each, thus it paid to sort carefully, and consign any fleece with a shorter or coarser staple to a lower grade, keeping No. 1 bale for only the top class wool.

The yearling lambs are usually shorn first of all, as their wool must be kept separate from the main flock: it has quite a distinctive character with a tip, never having been shorn before. The sheep due for shearing next morning must be put under cover overnight to avoid wetting by dew or rain.

I remember contriving a method of fastening the shearing shed doors, using an old iron bar and socket from the scrap-heap, adding a hasp and staple to take a padlock; for it is not unknown for wool thieves from Basutoland to come by night, pack fleeces into sacks, load them onto their ponies, and get across the border into their country before dawn. Here they would sell to unscrupulous storekeepers.

The shearers are happy to sleep all together in the engine shed or whatever building may be available. They are paid according to the number each has shorn. As each one finishes a sheep, he is given a bean which serves as a counter; this goes into his leather pouch attached to his belt. At the end he lays out all his beans in tens for ease of reckoning, and is paid what is due. In those years, now long past, the rate was ten or twelve shillings per one hundred sheep.

As each sheep was finished, it was pushed out of the door, after branding and dressing any chance cut with oil. The shearer immediately fetched himself another customer from the pen, and one of my own boys gathered up the fleece, throwing it expertly on the table, so that it landed spread out fully. It was immediately "skirted", dirty, short or hairy bits removed to join the locks, backs were taken out to go into a bale on their own, as they are always dusty and shorter; the length of staple was judged and tested for breaks, i.e., a thin line of weakened wool running through, denoting an illness at some time in the year. Such would demote the whole fleece to lowest grade. Should the length and crimp prove up to standard, the trimmed fleece, now almost uniform in length and texture, went into No. 1 bale. Umfaans spent the day tramping down the wool in each bale. The whole community took part, for women sat in a bunch picking over the locks as they were discarded on the floor, making sure no really scruffy bits should join the reasonable pieces which boasted a bale of their own. Everyone enjoyed the atmosphere in these few days of communal effort; and it was always a fine sight to watch a really skilled shearer stripped to the waist, the fleece falling at his feet, the sharply white body of the newly shorn sheep between his knees.

When all was done, the shearers were given an old sheep to slaughter for themselves before they went on to the next farm.

The bales were sent off by ox-wagon to the station, six miles away, for despatch to Durban and the Wool Sales. It was interesting to take the weights of the bales on the station scales before despatch, and hazard guesses as to what prices might be expected. After all, it was the one big cheque of the year, so all-important to the farm's prosperity. When the sheep had been restored to their respective camps, small baby lambs kept away from their mothers for ten hours and dosed, the shed restored to its normal use, and all dismantled and stored for another year, then our own boys were rewarded with a sheep for a celebration of the end of one of the chief landmarks of the farming year.

Those acquainted with sheep-farming procedure in England will know that wool-classing by the farmer himself, which is the rule in South Africa, is not so here. The fleeces are bundled up as they are shorn, and sent off without skirting. On the whole, the type of wool produced here is that grown by the mutton breeds, shorter and coarser than the very fine Merino wool which was favoured in the high country of East Griqualand.

Before leaving the sheep, I should touch on the feeling I had for them, and the enjoyment I found in all the essential dealings we had with them. Poor things, I could not help reflecting that almost everything we had to do for them, from the first tailing and castrating, must have been unwelcome, although essential to their survival.

We forced doses into them by means of a dosing gun, shooting it down their unwilling throats. This I usually did myself, as the Africans on the whole might not be meticulously accurate in the amount of medicine given individually. As the purpose was to combat internal parasites, the doses used contained strychnine or other poisons; too much could kill, too little fail in its effect. During the hot weather dosing had to be repeated at all too frequent intervals.

Another unwelcome event for the patient sheep was dipping, also vital to their health, but only carried out annually, a few weeks after shearing. This killed external parasites, known as keds, which lived in the thick base of the wool and sucked vitality from their hosts. For this, we were allowed to drive our flock over to a neighbour possessing a well-made sheep-dip tank. This was cement-lined and boasted a collecting kraal, a race or narrowly fenced run down to the bath, ending in a sheer drop to the circular pool, which gave the animal no chance to back-pedal on the edge as its companions pressed down behind, and finally a ramp leading up from the opposite side into a fenced concrete dripping yard. This was constructed with a good slope back to the dip, to allow the ked-killing liquid to run back into the tank. The sheep were held in this yard long enough for the copious amount carried out in their fleeces (acting as sponges), to be restored to sustain the necessary depth in the bath. We had to stand by with a long forked pole, which served to duck each sheep as it came up from its initial plunge, with a shrewd push on the neck. This ensured that even the top-knot was subjected to the treatment. As I used to stand carrying out this manoeuvre, I always thought of the clever foxes in this country, who are said to collect a lump of wool left by sheep on fences or twigs, carry it in their mouths, and immerse themselves in a pond or stream, leaving only the tip of their noses above the surface. As they emerge, minus their pests, the wool is dropped full of the fleas, which have sought sanctuary in this, the only dry harbourage.

Another vital task, which had to be carried out frequently and watched vigilantly, especially in hot, wet weather, was crutching, i.e., clipping the wool away round the tail and dressing the parts with oil to prevent infestation with maggots. The prevalence of the latter, the reason for tailing all lambs. None of these operations could have been welcome to the long-suffering sheep, although very necessary to their well-being.

One event I always enjoyed was counting the flocks, involving a ride down the Flats, and having the shepherd boy herd them into a corner and let them escape as gradually as possible, while I counted in two's, holding them back when a stampeded threatened. The whole scene appealed to me in that glorious setting, the hills beyond making a wonderful backdrop, while sheep and shepherd seemed part of past, present and future, and assurance for all time.

Dipping of cattle was a much more frequent task, carried out every two or three weeks in the hot weather, to kill the ticks which were picked up all too readily on the veld grass. We had our own cattle dip, built on the same lines as that for the sheep, differing in that the tank had to be long and rectangular, rather than circular, so that the cattle could not turn round and face the wrong way, and must swim a yard or so before reaching the ramp leading them out to the dripping kraal. The tank was sufficiently deep to ensure complete immersion at the initial dive. Most of the cattle, having been pushed in as calves, developed an admirable acceptance of the routine; realising the inevitability, they would leap in without hesitation to get the ordeal over with despatch. However, I remember the bull on one occasion presenting an amazing sight: he got to the extreme edge of the dip and refused to budge. He just stood stolidly, not protesting, just looking utterly immovable, with an unwinking stare straight to his front. Meanwhile, an army of boys got a rein round his quarters and tugged and pulled to collapse him forward; he remained passively resistant, not altering his expression until – suddenly, with a giant leap, he was in.

CHAPTER 20

Africans. Personal dealings

Through all these recurrent farm events, and weather ups and downs, there were many episodes with the Africans, which sometimes caused major disruptions and gave me temporary worries; but for the greater part gave much pleasure, interest, and indeed laughter, for they were a delightful, gay, happy people. Perhaps some of these happenings may be of interest, even to those who had not the luck to experience the life we shared with these simple, but large-hearted black people.

The farmer gives them unlimited mealie meal, which is the natives' natural food, and most give sugar also, any beasts that die on the farm, and an occasional gift sheep. Then, they get all the milk they want every week-end when separating is done, from this they make a sort of sour milk curd; in addition, usually they are allowed a daily whole milk ration when they have babies. Certainly, while working on the farms, they tend to fatten, and after a spell back at their own locations, they return very much thinned down. While on a farm, they get all kinds of everyday medicines from the farmer's wife, and the local doctors are very good about treating them for very moderate charges, and getting them to hospital free of charge if necessary.

The more intelligent, enlightened natives go to the white doctors readily, but many still trust in witch-doctors: although harm can come through them, so can much good. Their knowledge of herbs is deep, handed down from one generation to another. Remembering the extreme potency of mind over matter, the very presence of someone in whom they had faith could cure by suggestion alone. Abuses do not disprove the value. If they asked me to take them to a witch-doctor, or to fetch one to the kraal, I did not refuse, but by my readiness to support and help them to attain their imagined needs, they gradually came to have confidence, and faith that I could help them towards recovery, and if I wished them to go to a white doctor or hospital, more and more became willing. With each success and triumphant return from hospital, there were more converts to belief in the knowledge and skill of the whites.

Their simple trust in myself, ill-founded as it was, not on any practical knowledge or skill, when put to the test, found refuge in the psychological. There was a night when I had ridden over to a neighbour, and persuaded to sleep there, had decided to ride back in the early morning in time for milking. I had just gone to bed, when I heard a knock on my window (all farmhouses were single storied). I went to the window and found two of my own boys had ridden over to find me. They have an uncanny knack of knowing one's movements in detail! They had come to tell me one of the women was in labour and the baby would not come; would I return to the farm to help them? Of course, I said I would be with them as soon as I had dressed, and to save time, would they catch and saddle my horse (I expect it would have been two polo ponies, for I usually rode one and led another, which thereby exercised two and gave both companionship in a strange paddock).

Our little cavalcade was soon on its way through the dark night, myself and the two boys, four ponies in all.

I was all too conscious of my own ignorance in the matter of childbirth; I should have felt more at home with a ewe or a mare. However, at least I could get out the car if need be, and take the woman to hospital. In those war years, petrol was very scarce; I used horses almost exclusively, reserving the car for emergencies such as this. Having reached the farm, I left the boys to turn my ponies loose, and went into the hut where all the women of the farm were clustered round the patient. They made sounds of relief at my advent, luckily ignorant of my lack of experience.

Having satisfied myself that there was no obvious reason for the non-arrival of the baby, I decided to trust to the psychological before taking further steps. Accordingly, I told them that I would be in my cottage and would not go away again that night, that if all was not well in another hour, they must call me. I made up a vast jug of hot cocoa, which I took over to the hut as a comforting, relaxing agent; then prepared to spend the night in an armchair. Within twenty minutes, some of the women came over to tell me the baby was safely there.

Knowing I was on the farm, their trust in my readiness to help in whatever manner might be required, relaxed the tension, and immediately the baby was on its way.

The trust, humbling as it was, led to other occasions exemplifying the childlike nature of these endearing people. One day when the women were all out in the lands hoeing turnips, a picturesque line of colourful figures, their arms rising and falling in rhythm as they chanted in harmony (these people harmonise naturally, even as tiny children), there was an altercation between two of them. I was at the cottage and had not witnessed the incident, but the two came running down to me, accusing each other of having threatened with a knife. I sat them down, one on each side of the back door, and heard their complaints, the one against the other. I gathered it was a matter of jealousy, in which the husbands were involved, one fancying the other had been chasing her man, so I sent for the two boys. I told them seriously, it was a very bad thing, knives being involved, would they wish me to take the matter to the magistrate?

"No, no," they replied," you must tell us what to do."

Having heard both sides, I decided which was the more to blame, imposed some minor imposition in the nature of a fine on next month's wages, and off they all went, back to their work, singing, peace restored.

I am reminded of an episode illustrating the credulity or superstition that prevails among some of them. I was in my cottage in the dusk of early evening (twilight as we know it in England is unknown, the dark follows sunset so swiftly), when I was aware of a shadowy figure outside my window. Had it been one of my own boys, I knew he would have made himself known. This was a stranger, hesitant to come up to the door, yet wanting my attention.

I went out to greet him, and found him in obvious apprehension. He told me he was making his way to the next farm along the road, he had come far and now darkness had come down, and he was afraid. He feared the Tokolosh (a spirit credited with evil intent, or sometimes merely mischievous in character) and he could not make his way up the hill alone.

I told him the next farm was very close (a mere two miles), and once he reached the top of the hill, he would see lights at the huts beyond and below. Then I said I would come down to the road with him, and stand there as a guard, while he climbed to within sight of the huts where he meant to stay. Then he could keep his eyes on the lights (only flickering lanterns and glimpses of fires within the huts) and he would be perfectly safe. He seemed to accept my reassurance and set off with many backward glances to make sure I was safely there in the middle of the road.

He must have trusted my word in the end, for it was already too dark to see at any distance in the hollow. I waited until I could just make out his silhouette on the crest, where it showed up against the slightly paler sky. There he raised an arm as if in valediction, and I returned to the cottage, amused at the thought of myself setting up as a protector for this boy, a man much bigger and stronger than I was!

CHAPTER 21

Superstitions. Eclipse. Poison scare

Superstition plays a large part in their lives, and there were troubles among the boys when one was thought to be putting the evil eye, or an evil spell on some others. It might die down for a time, and then flare up again, having been simmering resentfully underneath. On one such occasion, the boy got across the others working with him on the wagon, and threatened them with a pitchfork. I felt I had to turn him out forthwith. He was polite and obedient and went quietly. I was sorry to lose him, as he was an intelligent boy and always well-mannered to me, but it was no good to have bad feeling on a farm, and I knew it was best to let him go.

It was quite common to find drunks among the boys on a Sunday night. There were two chief relaxations for them, racing their skinny native ponies, and having a good party, entailing the imbibing of much Kaffir beer (brewed by their wives from mealies). All through the war, when I was alone, they were extraordinarily good, trying their best to give me no trouble, only on one Sunday was I constrained to intervene. That night, quite late, some women came from the kraal in a great state of agitation. Would I come and deal with a big "Indaba" (trouble, in this case)? I found one of the boys very drunk, making a lot of noise, threatening to beat everyone up, too far gone for reasoning. However, my authority penetrated sufficiently for him to go off to his hut, as ordered. I said I would talk to him in the morning, and told the rest of the boys to stay with him, and hold him down if necessary. The women, I comforted by putting them together in a large hut, and assuring them the boy was under constraint.

Having been told by his jailors how he had behaved, the poor fellow was so deeply contrite next morning, I felt quite sorry for him.

He said, over and over again, how bad he had been to give me so much trouble when I was on my own. He was deeply ashamed of himself, and finally told me he would penalise himself, saying he would forego the races next week.

Other superstitions prevalent included such things as certain items of food considered allowable for women but not for me, or vice versa, such as eggs. An ox struck by lightning could not be touched by the boys; the women had to cut it up and carry it up to the kraal, where they could consume it with impunity, but not so their menfolk. They were all easily alarmed by strange phenomena.

When a total eclipse was imminent one year, I took care to warn them a few weeks beforehand, explained simply what would happen, and told them to tell all their friends and relations in the location, for we were close to the totality belt, where astronomers were able to make valuable observations. On the farm, we could see the moon's passage across the sun, but always a thin sliver of sun showed, and darkness was not quite complete. The most noticeable features were the strange, unnatural colours, half-light, and curious blurred outlines of shadows, although darkness was sufficient at midday for the animals to behave as if night had come, hens went to roost, sheep sped for the top of the hill where they always congregated for the night (warm air rises and nights at 5,000 feet were always cool).

A very sad occasion which threatened major disruption on the farm involved the severe illness of a boy, attributed by his relations to poison of unknown origin. I had feared appendicitis as he was in great pain, but found his temperature to be consistently low, sub-normal. His family would not hear of hospital or a white doctor in this case, it was Kaffir poison, they said, they must have a Kaffir doctor. At their request, I went to the location and fetched the witch-doctor they wanted. He performed his spells, and then went to fetch other medicines. In his absence, the boy asked for me. When I came into his hut, he managed to whisper a few halting words into my ear, but he was obviously far gone. His pulse was very faint. He said I could take him to the white doctor or even hospital.

So, I went to telephone to ask if I should move him in his condition, but before I could get through his relatives came to say I must not take him. I told them he had asked me himself, but they replied that that was only because he was so ill, he did not know what he was saying. I then consulted my reliable old house girl (who had been herself to hospital and had an operation done by a white doctor, and was usually able to convince the doubting), but she said I could not override the family; if they were adamant, I must leave him. If he should die, the doctor, the hospital and white medicine would be blamed for evermore; any confidence built up over the years would be lost. Two days later, the witch-doctor having tried further remedies without avail, I went into the boy's hut before breakfast and found him dying. I felt miserable, especially as he had asked me to take him, and wondered whether I fancied reproach in his look. After breakfast he was dead.

Not long afterwards, another boy was ill, and the Africans began to say that it must be due to the same poison which had killed Joel: on his deathbed he had prophesied that many more boys would die after him. They had buried him with appropriate ceremony, which always meant beer and a sheep to kill. They did not drink to excess, but I expect sufficient flowed to prime the surge of superstition and hysteria. Late at night, some boys came over to tell me there was an evil thing on the farm, this boy was very ill, rolling about in agony, they were all afraid and must leave. I knew that it was most unlikely that this illness should bear any relationship to that of Joel, and that, in all probability, it was due to a sudden surfeit of unaccustomed meat. However, it was none the less worrying.

I consulted the doctor on the telephone, describing the symptoms, then called all the boys together, explained the trouble as well as I could (finding the right words in Xhosa was often a difficulty), and told them it could have no possible connection with

Joel's illness. They calmed down that night, but even in the sober light of day, many said they must leave, they feared the evil.

However, some boys came asking for work, I took on one to fill Joel's place, then I sent to the most intelligent of my own boys and said that if they really meant to go, I must take on others forthwith, whereupon, somewhat sheepishly, he said, "I am staying." I guessed that would mean all would change their minds, and so it was. They none of them wanted to go, but had worked themselves into a state of agitation.

One day I had to sack a "big" umfaan (14–18 years, perhaps) owing to trouble with an intombazan, whose parents had complained. Next day, the other six came in a body to tell me they all wanted to leave. I gave them a long talk explaining the reason for sacking Machine, and why I could not have such doings on the farm. They listened quietly and, in the end, all said they wanted to stay. Off they went to their work, doing it extra well to show there was no ill-feeling.

Where tribal customs are involved, one cannot intervene, but in this instance, the parents had appealed to me, and I had felt bound to back them.

Incidentally, after a due time, Machine came back to promise me no further trouble, and I took him on again. When I went back to look at the farm after thirty years, now owned by a farmer I had known as a very little boy, the first "boy" still working there, now unrecognizably a big man with a beard, introduced himself as Machine, warmly welcoming me, telling me proudly he had worked for me. As soon as he said his name, of course I remembered. Hearing I was in the country, Africans came from over the mountains to see me, some I had known as small children, some told me their fathers or mothers had worked for me.

Very heart-warming it was.

These events stemming from fears or superstition need careful handling, and were a strain being alone, but eventually each episode probably cemented the relationship more firmly. There was much harmful fear yet certain planes on which these simpler, more primitive people touch spiritual worlds, are still beyond our comprehension.

CHAPTER 22

Numbers of Africans. Shelling. Thrashing.

The position of the South African farmer is patriarchal, living as he does surrounded by his flocks and herds, with a whole settlement of African workers and their families, which tended to include mothers-in-law, sisters, cousins, and many unspecified offspring. I remember an occasion when a smallpox scare necessitated general vaccination decreed by government. Lining up every native on the farm for the ordeal, I was amazed by the numbers I had been housing. Each one had been reported on arrival, permission asked for his or her "indawo". "Funa indawo" (literally, "want place" or lodging) is the recognised formula when the travelling native craves a resting place, but some seemed to have remained semi-permanently.

On the farm of 1,630 acres, our *official* total staff was six boys, i.e. men, four big umfaans, and three or four women in the house. Small umfaans (little boys) automatically herded cattle or sheep, wives, sisters and other spare women hoed or reaped, and helped in many ways with the innumerable odd jobs as the farm seasons came and went.

For all these Africans living on his farm, the farmer acts as guardian, doctor, confessor, mediator and advisor, but the loyalty and service and real "caring" he gets in exchange, in very many cases outweighs the farmer's part, or at least balances the scales.

The way in which the house girls soon learnt to rise to the occasion when visitors came for meals, expected or not, always gave us pleasure. They worked away with smiles, keen to put on a good show, and all would wash their clothes at the latest possible moment in order to be spotless. It always amazed me to see their enthusiasm for soap on the morning of a party. Their responsible attitude to their jobs was heart-warming. I remember taking my little cook-woman in to the doctor, who wanted her to go into hospital for a fortnight's treatment. She was an intelligent and enlightened woman, and said she would do whatever I thought right, her only anxiety apparently being the wish not to leave us cookless. So she asked to postpone the treatment a week while she taught her sister to take her place in the kitchen, saving me a lot of preliminary instruction.

There were several main farming events in their various seasons which involved the whole community: shearing, hay-making, thrashing and mealie-shelling. Some farmers, owning large farms, had their own machinery, but the majority such as ourselves made use of the travelling thrashers and shellers, which moved round from farm to farm in the appropriate season.

Usually, we had little warning of the imminent arrival of these contractors, we heard they had reached farms in the neighbourhood, then a message over the telephone told us they had finished at a nearby place and would be on their way to us within the hour. Feverish activity ensued, all the boys and every available woman, including the house girls, were alerted, and mealies on their cobs were bagged and brought out for tipping, packing needles and twine placed ready, and we were set. The machine arrived and the job began, the Africans enjoying the communal jollity which always attended these occasions, the children dodging to and fro among the bags or climbing on the ever-growing mountain of bare cobs. The boys poured the bags of unshelled mealies into the chute, and carried filled bags of grain to the women, who immediately stitched them up, having topped them to capacity.

The machine spewed out the empty cobs onto a vast heap and poured the grain straight into the bags placed in turn in position under the spout. It was a scene of non-stop activity while the machine was working, and when the job was finished, the women carried on stitching the last bags, while the boys carted them all to the store. A splendid sense of achievement at the end of the day was crowned with the reward of a sheep to slaughter, meat being the greatest treat for the African.

My part was counting the bags as the sheller was paid accordingly, and generally organising and overseeing. The machine produced roughly seventy bags of shelled mealies per hour. We selected a few bags of extra good grain for seed beforehand, taking the centre from the cobs (chopping off each end to go into the main lot), and putting the chosen parts through the sheller first. These of course were marked and set aside so a watchful eye was essential.

Thrashing meant much the same drill, the boys throwing the bundled oats on the escalator (removing the ties as they took up each bundle). Whatever yield we got at the end of the day was a bonus, for we sowed oats to be grazed as green feed, very valuable in the winter when little or no value remains in the frosted veld grass. We had not got the acreage to grow them as an arable crop for sale, but looked to all our plantings to provide feed for stock and Africans. Oats and barley were the usual green feed, mealies for silage and boys' rations, roots and pumpkins provided succulents for winter feeding. In addition a small acreage down to Lucerne could be cut several times in that climate, and made excellent silage very nutritious. The oats would have been grazed by the cows, then by sheep (the golden hoof, for they take it right down evenly and spread their manure equally well). If rain came regularly, the crop would come on again, and be grazed two or even three times, finally being left to make what grain it would, hence the bonus. In addition, we left 2,000 or so bundles unthrashed, which we fed to the horses complete, and the good old oxen got the straw from the thrashing.

CHAPTER 23

Veterinary details

Throughout the war, it was almost impossible to get a veterinary surgeon out to the farm. Petrol being in extremely short supply, farmers were allotted a ration geared to the distance from the nearest dorp or markets, but it had to be conserved with care against some sudden emergency such as transporting someone, black or white, to hospital. Accordingly, everything possible was done on horseback; not merely riding round the farm overseeing, but riding to the dorp for occasional shopping, to tennis, and to church, and of course to polo, and calls on friends. But vets also had a tight ration, and as in those days the nearest one to the farm was forty miles away at Kokstad, if you wanted him to come out you had to fetch him and take him back, 160 miles in all, using the bulk of your petrol in one go, not to mention paying for his time. It was quite literally cheaper to let the animal die if it must (unless you owned, say, a valuable imported bull, which we did not). Fortunately almost all farms were on the telephone, and advice could be sought from the neighbours or the vet himself by this means.

Very soon treatments for most of the common complaints, such as milk-fever, blown cattle or sheep, etc., became familiar, and having had a leaning towards veterinary practice all my life, it suited me well. It was easy to get supplies of all normally used serums and vaccines sent from Kokstad, and I did all the regular inoculations, e.g. blue-tongue in sheep, myself. In actual fact, never once did I have a veterinary surgeon on the farm, as all my farming was carried out in wartime, or in the period following the war, before conditions returned to times of peace. Nowadays there are vets in each farming locality, no longer such vast distances to cover, and no petrol shortage with which to contend, so it has become normal to call him in when necessary. However, I should have been sorry had I missed out on all the fascinating experience I had acquired of necessity.

Of course, many very primitive methods were used, now long superseded. For example, the treatment for milk-fever, which is due to a sudden demand on the calcium in the animal when the milk comes flooding in after the birth. An immediate massive injection of calcium gets the cow on her feet, but we had not reached that sophistication in those days. The approved method to which I resorted was to arrest the flow in of milk by temporarily immobilising the udder for long enough to allow recovery. This was done by pumping air into each quarter with the equivalent of a fountain-pen filler, and tying each teat tightly enough to keep the air in. The udder could not be left very long like this, but it served to stop the drain on calcium for a time to allow the cow to recover, and her system soon adjusted to the new conditions. Obviously, it was usually only the really heavy milkers which succumbed; we tamper with nature, breeding cows to produce many times the needs of one calf, and the natural adjustment is not equal to the influx. Somehow many, in fact almost all, milk-fever victims recovered despite these doubtful practices.

Blown animals were another frequent problem, due to excessive gorging on young green feed, especially Lucerne (usually a break-in, or occasionally lax herdsmen); death could follow in an incredibly short time unless immediate action was taken. If spotted in the early stages, a gag, in the shape of a thick piece of wood, tied firmly in the mouth, and a handful of salt thrown on the base of the tongue, to keep the tongue working, and the animal is kept on the move. With the mouth propped open the air is gradually expelled.

But if it has gone too far before being observed, the only answer is a trocar at once, or failing a proper trocar, a knife will do, and a judicious twist leaves enough passage for the air. I showed the boys, who might find themselves faced with such a situation, the place to stick in the knife, and of course the gag and salt drill.

I remember an occasion when, riding back from the dorp, I was met by a panting umfaan sent to hasten my return. Our best ox was down. This was Malhas, who pulled so hard no other ox could keep abreast of him in the yoke, he was always just ahead. He naughtily got in amongst the cows' turnips, and, with a guilty conscience, knowing he should not be there, just guzzled as hard as he could. When spotted by the boys, he had begun to blow up; they put in a gag, but he had gone too far, and fell down in the last stages. A boy stuck in a knife as instructed, but with little result. When I arrived, I found he had not left the knife in, but merely made a hole, so I jammed in a long dinner knife, and turned it to keep a good passage open. We got him up, and walked him about for some hours, but the poor old fellow was still pretty hoven, so I borrowed a neighbour's trochar, put it in, and eventually had to leave it in all night; this did the trick, but it had been touch and go.

While on the subject of disease, horse-sickness was a threat said to occur roughly once in seven years. Accordingly, when the anticipated time drew near, I was much on the alert for news of any victims in the neighbourhood. News came through of the odd case round Kokstad, then one or two belonging to nearer friends. Action was obviously vital, I had procured the vaccine in readiness, and inoculated all the polo ponies and farm hacks; at the same time, keeping all in from late afternoon until the sun was well up. The virus which causes the disease is thought to be transmitted by mosquitoes or other biting insects, which attack during those hours. I was lucky, and never had a case on the farm, but ours was a comparatively "safe" area.

Being in the foothills of the Drakensberg mountains, we always felt the great bastion of the range guarded us from attack by many of the pests which threaten farms in the great body of the continent, or down near the semi-tropical coast. When a plague of locusts was reported on its way, we never got more than a few stragglers, which got through somehow, the main swarm deflected safely.

The Berg, apart from its value as guardian and protector, was an ever-present glory. To ride to the top of Hill Camp and look across to the gleaming peaks, snow-clad even in high summer, gave a lift to the spirit, however low the previous mood. Since leaving South Africa, it is the mountains I miss more than anything, not only the Berg, but lower ranges such as the Mvenyane hills, always in sight from every point on the farm, providing a backdrop second to none for every scene – a span of labouring oxen, a shepherd boy massing his flock, a flight of geese rising from a pan in the middle distance.

Before leaving veterinary themes, there are other doings of that nature, occurring regularly, and thus becoming very familiar, de-horning calves, for example. When the "buttons", i.e., the knobs which will grow into horns, can be felt with a finger, they are cut with a sharp knife and the open place rubbed with a caustic stick, having taken the precaution of putting a thick strip of Vaseline or grease across above the eyes to make certain no caustic ran down there. Treated like this, the horns never develop; the calves appear to feel nothing after the first few minutes, they shake their heads and then tuck into their buckets. It is a far kinder method than de-horning when they are fully grown, a major operation, blood spouting until staunched with Stockholm Tar.

One day boys came to tell me they had found one of the young oxen lying dead. It had been perfectly well the day before; they said they could see no symptoms or signs of the cause. When an animal dies absolutely suddenly without warning, there is always the fear of anthrax, so I warned the boys they must not cut it up for eating until I had examined it, and I went down to take a blood slide to send for analysis. At the same time, I took boys with spades, as, if I could find no certain cause of death, I was going to make them bury it at once very deeply, and sprinkle with lime to take all precautions against infection, because of the anthrax possibility. However, when I got to the place, I found the top strand of wire in the fence broken, and unmistakable marks of fusing on the wire. The ox was lying close to the fence, so there was no doubt that it had been struck by lightning: we had had a very fierce storm the night before. The boys then sent their wives down to cut up the ox and carry up the meat.

They could not touch it, because, as I have indicated, superstition comes into it.

The herd bull, Jason by name of course, as the farm was called Golden Fleece, got a bad foot, which had to be poulticed for some days, and finally wedged up with the invaluable Stockholm Tar after all poison had been drawn out. He was an amiable fellow, and got so used to my ministrations, that I found I could even renew the poultice (made with bluestone and fresh hot cow dung, which draws and retains heat) out in the field, though at first obviously I tackled it with him penned firmly in the race. This latter was, as is common in this country, constructed of very sturdy timber, just wide enough to take the largest ox, or the aforesaid bull, but sufficiently narrow to make it impossible to right about turn – although I have memories of small heifers contorting themselves to that end, and becoming almost inextricably stuck in their efforts.

For the sheep, we made pens or folds (kraals), several together, intercommunicating with two way gates to make it easy to separate different groups after they had been mixed, say ewes from lambs. From these kraals, a race or crush, suited to their size, boarded rather than barred (as sheep have a talent for getting through impossible gaps), made dosing, castrating or tailing of lambs fairly simple. I have recollections of standing hour after hour dosing, handling each sheep in turn, the sun blazing down on the kraals, and looking longingly at the young trees we had planted round the folds, wishing they might sprout miraculously to give that shade for dosing which we planned for the future.

CHAPTER 24

Hay. Contour furrows. Farm events.

I have touched on the major events which occurred annually such as shearing, shelling and thrashing; but day by day farming brought a vast variety of tasks, part of the fascination of that unpredictable, never dull, rewarding life.

My part was of necessity largely the planning and overseeing. Good character building, as I had disliked organising and delegating, always preferring to get on with things myself. There I taught the boys to do everything possible, as it is bad for anything to be dependent on one person in case of unavoidable absence. A farmer's most important role is to keep an eye on every part of the farm, never neglecting one side while another is in the foreground. For example, it is too easy to leave the sheep for a few days while everyone is desperately busy hay-making, but it is fatal; one is sure to find they have got maggots, or started an epidemic of blue-tongue during that brief interval. Certain intricate tinkering with machinery, riveting, etc., I would do myself, but the boys learnt more and more, and I could leave a lot to them as time went on.

Haymaking, for which we grew a special grass called "teff" (veld grass had not the value for feed), could feature more than once in a season, and, like most things, could present problems. In a normal summer, we could expect a daily rain round about four o'clock each afternoon. The heat of the sun until that hour was strong enough to dry the previous day's cut sufficiently, and allow time to rake it up and get it safely cocked before the storm. Difficult to credit, thinking of conditions over here. However, there were occasions when it was not so simple. Cutting the teff itself can be difficult, for it is a very fine feathery grass and it lies down flat under the least provocation, which makes it desperately hard to cut. The mower cannot go through cleanly, but keeps getting clogged and tangled up. The only thing to do is to rake the teff in one direction, so that it all lies the same way, and then take the mower through in the opposite direction, getting the blade in under the overhanging grass so that it cuts the stems. By no means as easy as it sounds, there would be constant stoppages.

After a heavy cloud-burst, the grass would be not only lying down, but seemed battered into the ground; sometimes we had to abandon part altogether, summon all the women and cut with sickles, a slow business. On other occasions, heavy rain in place of the usual fairly moderate storm in the afternoon, would arrive just too soon, and catch us before we had time to cock the hay. All would have to be spread out once more, turned, and dried out from scratch all over again. It could be a heart-breaking job, just as it can be here.

Sometimes planting could be a headache when drought or other weather hazards prevented the start at the approved time; this resulting in a wild rush, following the ploughs with harrows, the harrows or cultivators with planters, and probably continuing the same sequence for a different crop, without a break. A wet-day job (among many) was the mending of hoes, newly contrived handles in most cases. I would muster 15 to 20 in all, then as turnips reached a stage when hoeing was indicated, out came the women, and soon I would have a brave array of damsels working away in line, chanting with lovely harmonies as they went. It was a fine sight to see them swinging in rhythm, their singing most attractive, especially coming across the lands and veld from a distance.

Contour furrows were a vital necessity where storms could be so violent, severe soil erosion was inevitable without this protection. These are strips of unploughed turf following the natural contours of each "land" at intervals across the whole, the breadth of ploughed soil dependent on the steepness of the slope, the steeper the narrower of course, and the more furrows. I was able to borrow a theodolite to mark the line, and, as we pegged it out, a single-furrow plough followed the line before any pegs could be displaced, then returned throwing the turf the opposite way, leaving a yard or so unploughed between the two furrows. For this plotting for a new land on an occasion during the visit of a cousin (due to temporary sojourning in Durban, where a naval husband had a shore job during the war), I had the enthusiastic help of a young daughter with a most useful practical bent. Two people were essential, and on other occasions, I got the ready assistance of neighbours, sometimes going over to another farm to do duty in the same way for them in return.

When I went to a really successful well-run farm, I used to feel there was nothing in the world I wanted so much as to build up such a place. The care of the soil most obviously underlined, furrows well made up and kept up, splendid tilth. The stock a joy to look at, a beautiful herd of high-producing cows, lovely Afrikander oxen, big well-grown sheep. Cow shed, dams, dips and other structures all well planned and carried out, such satisfaction throughout.

Talking of Afrikander oxen, these beasts were the very best type of working ox in the country. Strong and good doers, they can keep fit on poor fare in an amazing way. They are good to look at, too, all red with a small hump. A team of these grand fellows, twelve, fourteen, sixteen, all pulling with a will, was a splendid sight. I shall not forget the day I got my first pair, a start towards that longed-for team.

While speaking of odd farm events, the vital windmill, which normally found enough breeze to keep the tanks topped up, supplying water to the kraal for cows, and also to the house, could fail in a long windless period. On one occasion, an extra-long failure from the breezes reduced us to dipping buckets in a muddy spring, and boiling all drinking water. When this became an intolerable burden, and still no sign of a breath of wind, I set the boys on to disconnecting the pumping apparatus from the wheel, fixed two handles and put a couple of boys on to pumping by hand, squatting one each side at the base.

They worked away for a time, but when it became both tiring and boring, I found them easing off, gazing at the heavens, and whistling continuously. When I questioned them, and was about to indicate a return to pumping was required, they told me they were whistling for the wind. Either their faith was rewarded, or coincidence provided a miracle, for in a very short time, the first waft was felt, and soon a real gale was blowing, which continued for days. We hurriedly connected up the main shaft once more, stored the handles against another great calm, and the wheel spun merrily, indeed soon it was creaking and straining in the blast. The tanks were refilled very quickly, and the overflow gaily supplying all subsidiary containers. Triumph for the whistlers!

CHAPTER 25

Evacuees

Sometime after the Second World War had begun, many Forces' wives, widows and families, who had been in Egypt, Singapore or other stations in the Middle East were sent down to South Africa for safety, out of the immediate war zone. These were largely placed in hotels on the Natal coast. Some had husbands who were prisoners in the P.O.W. camps, some were missing or killed, most of these families had been offered a choice of repatriation to Britain, or a sojourn for the duration in India or South Africa. Those choosing the latter felt that being still in the continent of Africa, vast though it is, they were perhaps closer to the war in the Middle East for a possible and longed-for reunion eventually.

Several farmers' wives, in East Griqualand, whose husbands were not involved in the war, offered to have some of these families in turn, up to the healthy heights, where they could recover from Natal sores, and other troubles due to the semi-tropical climate on the coast. This was an effort to do something towards helping in the War.

Some farmers had gone to join the forces in the Middle East, a few, like my husband, who had been a Regular, were on the Reserve of officers, and were called up as the first hint came, the phoney war, the Munich crisis in 1938. In most cases, a neighbour or relative took over temporary management for those who had gone.

In my case, a near neighbour, over age, and his son (under age until later, when he went, and was killed) were only two miles away, and ready to help and advise, so I stayed on my own and found much satisfaction in running the farm. Another splendid farmer in the district, who had slept under his wagon in his early days, while starting to build up a first rate farm, constituted himself my mentor, and found himself consulted on many problems in my own early days.

After some three years alone, except for my children in the holidays, I was invited to ride over to one of these hospitable farms, some six miles away, to meet an R.A. F. wife with two small children, up from the coast for a short break. She hailed from England, and her hosts thought she might like to meet someone from the same country.

She was told in advance that I had hunted in England, my horse interests being well known by then. She of course pictured a hard-bitten horsey woman, as portrayed in certain caricatures, and thought I might not be in her line at all. However, as we surveyed each other across the dining table, she felt she had seen me somewhere before.

After lunch she asked me whether I had ever gone to help with the Games staff at the Royal School in Bath, and started them playing lacrosse. They had been a hockey school, but their staff was keen to get them going with "lax". She and I had both played for the Wiltshire Ladies after I had left Cheltenham, hence the request, to which I was delighted to accede. My new R. A. F. acquaintance had been a girl at the R. S. at the time, so had come in for some of my instruction.

Thus we met again on a remote farm, and I soon discovered she had always longed to ride, so I asked her to come and stay with me. I mounted her on my daughter's steed; there was no doubt of her delight in it, and indeed in all farm doings.

She had imaginatively managed to get herself with her children and the Nurse into a cottage belonging to the hotel where she had been placed. It made a more normal life for them, and running the cottage gave her occupation, so necessary in those sad days, when she was still hoping that any day, she might hear that her husband had returned.

He was W/Cmdr. Paddy Coote, a first-rate pilot and a rugger international, having played for Ireland, posted Missing during operations over Greece. Muriel could imagine his plane brought down in the mountains of Albania, and himself perhaps sheltered in a very remote area; this hope continued for a long time, becoming ever more faint. Alas! she never heard to this day, the strain and sadness of that time for her can only be imagined.

Not long after our meeting, the hotel wanted the cottage, and she was given notice. I suggested she might care to come to the farm, which, to my great advantage, she did, as she threw herself into the life, helped me with everything, dosing sheep, checking cattle, learning to class wool. Nobly she took over the ordering of meals; until then I had often been pursued onto the farm by my small cook-girl, asking what she could cook for lunch, and I, with my mind on sheep or cows, would say unhelpfully, "Whatever you can find," and ride off. Poor Regina, at this distance, I do sympathise. Muriel changed all that, quickly learnt a few key words of Xhosa, and splendidly tackled the housekeeping problems, leaving me blessedly free for my farming.

She and the native girls had many laughs over her struggles with the language, but they understood one another well enough, even when I heard her urging Regina to put "wind" into a soufflé, the only Xhosa word she knew which seemed at all apt!

The help she gave me, not least companionship, was without price; I could only hope that perhaps all the new interests, and unending occupation, in a small way helped her through that agonizing, anxious time. She and Paddy had always thought a farm background would be ideal for young children growing up, absorbing naturally many of the lessons such as births and deaths, which have to be accepted eventually, Thus she felt this was what he would have wished for her and them in this sad crisis.

CHAPTER 26

Drakensberg ride

One year when winter was almost over, but before spring rains were due, heralding the usual ploughing, planting, etc., progression of vital work, it was possible to plan a break for a few days. We knew the boys would keep up the daily routine of feeding stock, and could be trusted to keep an eye on all sheep and cattle; should there be any trouble, they could be instructed to report to my good neighbour. Thus we felt justified in absenting ourselves for a short time.

We had often heard stories of how in the old days, when buses and railway were unknown, men had covered enormous distances on horseback. Why should we not do the same in a minor way? We would undertake a really long ride. So we marshalled our saddlebags, a normal item in use whenever riding in to the local dorp. These would take all small things for our great trek, and anything we should need en route. We contrived a pack on an old saddle with special surcingle to carry our bulky needs. This took a lot of fixing to get the balance just right.

Muriel rode her favourite Jower, I took a failed polo pony called Harmony, passed on to me by Tommy Pope (top handicap polo player for South Africa), who felt he would never make it on the field. With this I agreed, but I had been asked to find a riding pony or farm hack for someone in the Kokstad area, so thought if I took him on this long ride, I should know all there was to know about him, in case he proved to be the answer for my customer. Rima, the foal that had been born when her dam was lent to us on that first farm where we started our care-taking, was our packhorse. I had broken her in myself, and she had become my daughter's property, as related elsewhere. She was utterly reliable, and though never brilliant, had proved herself a sensible character. I knew she would accept the strange load without question. I led her throughout, she never hung back, merely nipping my knee occasionally at the end of the day when we were all tired!

So we set out, having adjusted everything with care, as we thought, and with a good send-off from all the Africans. A kind neighbour had offered hospitality to Muriel's children and nurse in our absence.

We had not progressed more than half a mile before the pack slipped, despite all our efforts to balance it exactly. We were forced to halt, unpack the lot, and reassemble from scratch, Rima patiently enduring the process. This time, we triumphed, and it never slipped again all through the trek. I found I had to get to it first each morning after a night's stop at the farm of some friend or hospitable stranger, ever ready to help with our preparations, but having discovered the knack of securing the load against all the hazards of rough and sometimes rocky terrain, we felt safer if we had fixed it ourselves.

We found with a led packhorse, and the need to off-saddle in the heat of the day to give the horses a feed and a rest, not to mention ourselves, we only covered about twenty-odd miles a day. Accordingly, we stopped at various farms three separate nights en route. This enabled us to let the horses loose in a paddock for some grazing, albeit only winter veld, but our kind hosts invariably contributed some hay, and we were able to replenish the small bags of oats we slung from our saddles for the midday feeds. We ourselves, were treated with the generosity to be found on almost every farm in the locality, being given an evening meal and royal breakfast before we set off at six or seven o'clock.

We were heading for a place high up in the Drakensberg mountains, roughly ninety miles from Golden Fleece, thus we were climbing fairly steadily, though not always perceptibly, occasional steep scrambles eased out for some miles before we came to another assault. We knew our general direction, but as we travelled cross-country as far as possible, we had to question each of our nightly hosts as to where we might find gates through farm boundary fences which would have held us up. Often it was necessary to break out onto a farm track, or a road for a spell, as most farm boundaries were double-fenced and fairly impregnable. These detours, of course, added considerably to our total mileage, impossible to estimate exactly other than by totting up the hours on the move. We knew we covered no more than four miles an hour, often less with our packhorse in tow, and the rough ground encountered on the way.

Setting out in the glorious early mornings, the sun just beginning to banish the cold of night; yet the air still fresh, cool and invigorating, it was an inspiring sight to view the next distant range of the mountain, knowing that by evening we should have reached or even passed that horizon.

When we reached our goal, an hotel patronised by Johannesburg and Durban trout-fishermen, or those needing some mountain air after the accustomed heat and humidity of the coast, we found most bedrooms were rondavels, which made a pleasant refuge from the main hotel.

We had counted on some grazing of good new grass here; so high in the mountains spring rains come early, and sure enough the "burns" on the hillside were greening over already, although at home we had left the farm still in its winter garb. We had not even been able to burn, as rains still seemed far off.

We arranged to put our three horses in a paddock near the hotel for the nights, and we found an umfaan willing to herd them on the mountain slopes by day. He led them up there, then left them loose to graze, seated himself on a mound, and simply hurled a clod deftly if one or other strayed too far. Such is the usual method of herding; the urchin invariably develops incredible skill so that the clod lands just beyond the errant animal and startles it back in the required direction.

We allowed the horses a few days complete rest, thereafter, exploring with them the country roundabout. Relieved of leading our packhorse, and unencumbered with feed bags and other impedimenta, we felt gloriously free to wander in that wonderful scenery at whatever pace we fancied, or the ground dictated. I remember climbing single-file up a steep cleft in the mountain, marked out by a rushing stream, which we had to trust our steeds to avoid at some peril. They had become adept at navigating the boulders and rocky outcrops during this great trek, so we gave them their heads and they carried us safely up to our target. This was a curiously shaped vast rock protruding over one side of the gorge, looking like a huge hooded monk, brooding over the wild scene. Someone had told us of The Monk, so of course we had to find him. Picking our way down the gorge was more difficult than climbing up, however, we had faith in our mounts, and simply tried not to hamper them by any sudden shift of balance.

When we emerged onto the open mountainside, we were glad to knee-halter them so they could graze, while we tackled our sandwiches in bliss. Some days I rode Rima to give her a turn, leaving Harmony in our small herd's care; Muriel kept to her Jower, always the chosen one. A few days of freedom such as this gave us a perfect break.

Reluctantly, we bade farewell to our little herd-boy, loaded up our packhorse once more, and set our faces for East Griqualand, another ninety miles ahead. We were still high in the mountains when a cloud came down on the shoulder where we rode. We were in thick mist and could see nothing to guide us. We searched about, hoping to see a sign of a track, but soon realised we had lost all sense of direction. So we let our reins slack on our horses' necks and trusted them to find the way, heading towards home as we were. They carried us unerringly. Suddenly we were down out of the mist, and there below was the whole glorious country bathed in sunlight, the gateway off the mountain just at hand.

We took a slightly different route on our homeward way, staying the nights at other farms. Tiring of leading her, I sometimes let Rima loose to follow us, knowing she would naturally head for home, but not want to be too far away from the other horses. She amused us when she thought she knew best and occasionally went off at a tangent, tossing her head and obviously saying, "*I* know the right direction, it's this way." Certainly, she did, but she did not know we had been told the only gate through a boundary fence, which soon came to view, was on the route we had taken. Seeing us persisting in our diversion, eventually she would come cantering up, her packs bumping her flanks, and push in between our two steeds, feeling a bit stupid, we thought, but anxious to keep her end up.

When we got back, we plunged straight into the busiest time of year on the farm, but refreshed and quite ready to take up the reins once more. It had been a great experience; one we shall never forget.

CHAPTER 27

Great Dane

For nine years, I had the companionship of a perfect dog. This was Griselda, Zelda for short, a brindle Great Dane bitch. We had often thought of the dog we should have when we settled on our own place – impossible to have one while moving from farm to farm. I had always longed for a Great Dane ever since, aged five, gazing at the picture of Little Lord Fauntleroy with his arm round the neck of his grandfather's Great Dane, just the perfect height, I felt.

Here it seemed the ideal breed, the size and deep bark makes him alarming to strangers and therefore an excellent guard; I thought I should not mind at all being left alone on the farm with such a companion (so soon to be put to the test, though utterly unexpected at the time). Then the daily rides round the farm would be excellent exercise, their short coats and good clearance are great advantages in that country, where it is always either extremely dusty or extremely muddy. They are so quiet and dignified that their size is not an inconvenience, and once they are full-grown, they eat less than the sporting breeds (setters and Labradors, etc.). Altogether, I was longing to have one; we kept our ears pricked but had no luck. Once we came near it when we heard of a bitch with nine puppies, crossbread with a Bull-mastiff, but when we went to see them, they had all just died from a form of dog influenza.

Then our luck was in. We went to spend a night on the farm where we had lived for our first few months in the country. Here we found one Mrs. Lloyd from Mooi River staying there also. She was acknowledged the leading breeder of Great Danes in the county at the time, expecting at least fifteen guineas for all her puppies! It would now be more like a hundred and fifty, forty-five years later. She had with her Garry, her stud dog, many times champion, the most glorious specimen I had ever seen, with perfect gentlemanly manners. He was brindled and huge. My envy must have been apparent.

We talked Great Danes a good deal during the weekend. Finally on the Sunday, Mrs. Lloyd took me aside and said she would give me a bitch puppy, very like Garry. It seemed too good to be true (at fifteen guineas, we never thought we could hope to own one). I could hardly find words to accept. She then explained that she did not keep bitch puppies, unless there were so few dog pups in a litter that she had to keep one or two for the sake of the mother. The few bitches thus kept, she would not sell, as people might breed from them from inferior stock, and then use her name to sell the puppies and spoil her reputation and market. So occasionally, she used to give one to people she could trust to appreciate the dog and not attempt to breed in opposition. Needless to say it was not difficult to assure her I was more than ready to carry out her conditions.

Shortly afterwards, we drove up to Mooi River in Natal, to Mrs. Lloyd's most interesting farm. The country there is very beautiful, having far more trees than East Griqualand. The whole district is outstanding for beauty in scenery, imposing well-built homesteads, and accessibility to Pietermaritzburg civilization, hence, many settlers are lured thither. However, we were glad to have had farming experience before seeing these charms, or we might have fallen for them in ignorance. With farmers' eyes we could see the snags, and realised that the country, which could make an ideal home for the retired man wanting a hobby, is not the land for farmers who must make a living. Despite the obvious attractions, we could not think of farming seriously there; soil is poor, sorrel was rife, and grazing sour, being in the mist belt. In addition, wages seemed very high compared with the rate then accepted in East Griqualand: in those days farm boys got fifteen shillings a month, house girls ten, whereas in Natal the equivalents were twenty-five to thirty, and house-boys twenty-five to fifty for a good cook-boy. These rates must sound incredibly low now.

The very fact of Maritzburg's accessibility is another disadvantage to a farmer who wants to do well on his farm. It is impossible to be in a town for even a few hours without spending money. It was far better to be out of reach generally, and have to improvise one's needs; certainly, I welcomed the main grocery order, once in six months, rather than the almost daily, or at least weekly shopping that seems to be necessary over here.

Mrs. Lloyd was the widow of a Gunner General, who came to Natal on retiring. Her married daughter and retired Indian Army husband lived with her. The two latter ran poultry on a large scale, and also the garden; Mrs. Lloyd herself kept her hand on the reins of the whole farm, aided by a Dutch manager. Her chief lines were pigs and Great Danes, for each of which, by trial and experiment, she had worked out the most economically successful balanced ration. She was the leading pig breeder in the district, and the local creamery had put her in charge of the piggeries which are run in connection with the factory. A very successful show it was. She was also on the Management Board of the Bacon Factory in Natal. To all this she had attained through her own efforts and serious study of the problems. She was a fine woman with a commanding personality. Her farm was full of improvements, ideal buildings and contrivances, but she had to buy nearly all her feed, whereas we in our area all aimed at being self-supporting from our own land.

We spent two nights there, inspecting the whole farm, the creamery, the piggeries, a local stock sale, even a flower show; then we started back to Golden Fleece, taking with us the perfect puppy. She surpassed every dream of mine, a beautiful brindle with huge paws, a black muzzle and lovely domed head. Already her bark was deep, and she had great natural dignity. We named her Griselda: it suited her perfectly. She accepted us very quickly, settled down happily and quite lost her anxious expression.

For our return journey, we ventured on the so-called wild road from Mooi River to Underberg, which goes through glorious country, close under the Berg the whole way. It was risky, as some of the hills can be hazardous in rain; there is often a sheer drop on one side with absolutely nothing to prevent skidding over the edge. We were more than glad we had risked it; the country was worth many hair-raising moments, of which we had plenty, for a sudden storm provided the greasy surfaces we had hoped to avoid.

CHAPTER 28

Horses on the farm

It would seem right to record something of the many horses which came to me on the farm, some were outright gifts, some as payment for schooling one or two ponies, some bred on the place, others on loan while their owners went to the war. All were welcomed, most had marked characters, each was an individual.

The story of our first three, Pip, Rima and Con, has been told in Chapter 16; these moved with us to our own farm. Very soon horses began to multiply. Almost immediately, I was given a mare that had played good polo but was then unsound for hard galloping though a delightfully comfortable hack. She had a certain amount of quality, and had been named Nomis, as St. Simon figured in her pedigree. The idea was that I should attempt to breed from her, her own proficiency at polo and her breeding warranted the hope that she might produce something useful. Unfortunately, she had not been bred from in her youth, which would have made the proposition more hopeful; she failed to get into foal. However, she gave me a deal of pleasure as a hack, her fine coat which testified to the thoroughbred in her being a constant delight, and her amazingly smooth paces a comfort on any long ride. Her late owner used to say you could sit her at a gallop with a jelly on your head.

I looked at the four horses in the paddock with much the same feelings I had had as I gazed at Tip-top and Joe over the stable doors. Could this be true? Farming at its earliest beginnings and already a stud assembling, at no cost at all, save those nominal figures for the children's steeds, paid from their own small savings. Here were our mounts for all farm doings requiring a horse; Pip carried a native into the nearest dorp on the rare occasions when we felt news from home justified taking someone from the clamouring farm-work. Whenever I could find an odd moment, I began Rima's early training.

Having got through the first summer with all its urgent work, we came to autumn and the start of polo. A most generous neighbour lent us two ponies, so we were able to get a real stable going, sleep them in and play once a week.

During the preliminary period before finding Golden Fleece, when we were moving round caretaking on different farms, at each and every one we found mounts of a kind. When the owner was a polo-playing farmer, there were his ponies to be ridden, and much interest in the handling; and when the only farm hack proved to be a real hairy, kind neighbours lent a pony recently up from the Cape, where she had played polo and been hunted with the Cape Hunt. So I was fortunate, and discovered early the extraordinary kindness and generosity of the whole community, where everyone is not only ready but goes out of his way to help with practical assistance, gifts from farm or garden, or advice.

Surely Tip-top and Joe had set the ball rolling, well and truly, and it was not to stop. Thinking through the string of horses that came and went during my time in South Africa, I have lost count of loans or temporary members of the stud, apart from young ones sent to me for schooling, sometimes animals with some pet foible would come to try to forget it.

Names crowd in and each and every one is attached to some particular tag (or should it be reversed?). There were Atalanta and Apollo, both out of the same dam, both, alas! showing the same failing, a complete lack of "snap." Big and comfortable, pleasant in nature, but so sticky that it was real hard work to fling Atalanta round a polo field at all, and in the game, she was maddening, never quite getting there in time. No amount of schooling really woke her up; she was allowed to breed a foal eventually, when it was accepted she would never make a polo pony, but could produce a useful farm hack, such as Pip. Only once do I remember her thoroughly on her toes, and then it was a bit too dashing. Tied to a rotten branch of a tree by an unthinking African, she threw her head, the branch came away on the end of the rope, and she was off, terrified by that cracking, banging, rustling thing at her heels, which took great bounds with every one of hers. She went flat out across the first land and slap through five strands of barbed wire fencing at which she never rose at all, but took broadside. Amazingly, it hardly checked her mad flight; she kept on for a mile and a half before a collection of natives at the cheese factory stopped her. Her legs came up like drain-pipes all round, and she was a sorry sight for some weeks. Despite her unsatisfactory record, it was gratifying, a year later, when she was sent to stud at another farm in the locality, that on getting out of her paddock at night, she came back to me instead of making for her real home; I feel she bore me no grudge for all the hard work into which I had pushed her, hustling her against her nature unmercifully.

If Atalanta was sticky, her half-brother Apollo was stuck! He was the clumsiest horse I have ever come across, and quite appallingly heavy in hand. Twenty minutes on Apollo trying to get him to place his feet even reasonably was utterly exhausting. If he could put his feet wrong, he would, and could tie himself into incredible knots. Three times he fell down flat in the training kraal, literally falling over himself. As I led him out to the paddock, he would frequently tread on the backs of my heels or stub his toes against anything. He blundered and stumbled and just could not raise enough interest to look what he was doing, to think at all. The only way to get any semblance of response out of him was to shake and push him into a flat-out gallop, then before he had got over the surprise of finding himself in a hurry about anything, there were a few moments when, in spite of himself, he got around with a little dispatch. But he soon lapsed back to his accustomed lumbering roll, and all hope of inspiration was gone. His owner soon sold him as a riding horse, and I believe he carried a native priest on his rounds, and a very comfortable hack he would have made, provided there was no hurry. A nice friendly fellow, and up to any amount of weight.

Sorbonne was a little mare, full of quality and speed: no horse has given me greater pleasure to ride. I have never known one quicker in reaction or more nippy on her feet. She could handle herself beautifully and was sheer joy to school, but she had come off the race-course with the habit of jibbing when over-excited, and nothing broke her of it. Though weeks would go by without any manifestation, she could never be relied on not to start it up again in moments of over-stimulation. For weeks I schooled and rode her, enjoying her more than any, and getting wonderful response, but on the polo ground in the middle of a chukka, back would come the old trouble. She would stand rigid and trembling, head up, and eyes staring like a mad thing. Sometimes it would last as much as five minutes before she would break the trance, fling herself round a half circle and off. No punishment had any effect, indeed it merely prolonged the resistance; calm encouragement by voice was the only answer,

Hack races and polo pony scurries at a local gymkhana tempted me to try her once more in a race. If only she would start, she should have it all her own way. She was outwardly calm in the paddock before the race, though inwardly strung up taut. She went down to the start on her toes, and I longed to get her off without a hitch, for she felt fit to gallop away from the lot. However, the nervous tension at the start was too much for her. I tried to keep her moving quietly while the starter gave his orders, and having an outside position, was able to circle gently till the last moment, but coming into line finally, the excitement and memories of previous experiences on the race-course overcame her, she went rigid. The rest of the field were off. I had to bite back my exasperation at the sight of those fast-disappearing tails, as I leant forward and pulled her ears, encouraging her to pull herself together. Suddenly she responded, with a colossal bound we were off, and fairly flying after the field with such a burst of speed, I almost thought we should catch them, but the distance was too short to allow us to overhaul them, though she made up an incredible amount and gave me the gallop of a lifetime.

Once more I tried her, hoping perhaps, having got her off at all on a race-course, the spell might be broken, but the start was the same, though she put up such a terrific run that she was never to lose altogether. She gave me as much pleasure as any horse I have ridden, and a great deal more than most. Had I been in a position to buy any horse, I should have loved to have owned her. Indeed, I went to the sale where her owner put her up, hoping she might go for a song, longing to be able to buy her in, but it was not to be. In actual fact, I never bought a horse except when commissioned by other people, until my very last year in the country, when I put a birthday cheque into the purchase of a country pony of a very useful type, that schooled into a most reliable hack, made a useful gymkhana pony, was in constant demand for all and sundry, and, though never brilliant, went into practice polo, played a quiet game and gave confidence to beginners. He turned out to be a good speculation, his value going up considerably. Apart from that aspect, he was a very good friend and most satisfactory family pony; just the type for many in England today.

A couple of young ponies came to me for breaking and schooling. In payment for my work on them, I acquired a chestnut gelding, Shumar, by repute part-Arab and badly broken. Certainly, he had had his nerve spoiled by some mishandling, and he never got over his terrors of innumerable real and imaginary things. Any ride on Shumar was liable to be exciting, for he could do such rapid right-about turns, you would find yourself off at a gallop in the direction whence you came, before you had time to realise anything had happened. He could get himself about so well that he might have been a brilliant performer on the polo ground, if only he had not so many fears. Poor fellow, he was terrified of everything. I schooled him for hours with stick and ball, hitting it against a wall, having it coming back at him from all angles, till he really could stand up to it without flinching; but on the polo field, among all the other players, he said plainly, "I don't mind when you hit it, but what about all those other people? They might do anything!"

He would frequently shy off the ball or an oncoming opponent. Nevertheless, I played him three chukkas a week for two seasons and had lots of fun, some excitement, and plenty of exasperation. Like many another, he preferred to lead with one leg to the exclusion of the other, so I purposely put him off on his unaccustomed leg as often as possible. He was clever in his attempts to get back on to the other one, for finding that I always noticed immediately if he made a direct change, and changed him straight back again, he would pretend to shy at some imaginary object, and getting into his stride again after the break, off he would go on his favourite leg. He would do this over and over again, but I was relentless. A big strong chap, showy chestnut with a good deal of white, he was always fun to ride, and made a splendid mount over a distance, but he never lost his fears, and was always liable to be a nuisance, breaking bridles, ropes, etc., in sudden paroxysms of terror.

The two young things whose training earned me Shumar, though both by the same sire, a thoroughbred, could not have been more different from each other; one being stolid, stocky, in build and temperament, quiet to handle from the start, but never to show any brilliance. He soon went off as a farm hack, any polo pony schooling an obvious waste of time. The other, Kashmir, as highly strung and quick as her half-brother was slow, gave me plenty of thrills during her training, coming over on top of me when putting in a buck on a steep slope, and requiring a good deal of sobering in a ploughed field, where she tired into a reasonable frame of mind, and at least it was soft to fall. She handled as well as any I have known, and had plenty of intelligence, and though she could set herself against you in sheer devilment, she knew what was wanted all right, and when she gave in, her response was perfect. She turned into one of the very best ponies in first class tournament polo, finding her way eventually to the stables of a well-known Johannesburg player.

Among the many horses which became part of our stable for a shorter or longer time, some made an indelible mark on my memory, while others faded as time went on.

Junisa, a thoroughbred mare, given to me as a brood mare by an interesting retired veterinary surgeon from Basutoland (in fact father of the intrepid girl, who rode her stout Basuto pony, Sincipatu, to the top of Mt. Currie with me as related in Chapter 10), was definitely one of those never to be forgotten. A charming character, and the most delightful of rides. Though no longer sound enough for polo, or marathon expeditions, she was almost my favourite mount for local or farm hacking. She bred me a lovely colt foal, Juror, by the favourite stallion Reckoning Day. This foal was sold on into one of the top polo stables of Johannesburg; unfortunately, I left South Africa too soon to follow his subsequent career.

Another very favourite mare, with whom I had a very special link, was Viv. (Her name was the only thing about her that seemed wrong to me, Vivian. She was not mine, alas! so Viv it had to be.) She came to me "for the duration" from one of the elite Jo'burg players, so had to return when he came back from the war. She could do anything, not only on the polo-ground, where she taught me a great deal, but she won a polo pony scurry in record time, a bending race on the same day, thus coming back to supreme control immediately after the excitement of a flat-out race, and finally helping me to victory spearing a dangling ring at full gallop. She was a joy at any pace, and showed an uncanny sympathy with my feelings. Let loose at the hundred-acre hill camp with a bunch of others, it was their wont to gallop to the top of the hill, bucking and glorying in their freedom, but I have known her check in the first few yards, return to me at the gate, muzzle me and tell me plainly she knew something was troubling me, walking beside me with intermittent nudges of understanding, instead of joining the wild skelter to the top. Several times, she feigned lameness when someone else got on for a ride; if I took over to try locate the trouble, she went sound instantly, and no further signs ensued. Curious, but true, as vouched for by the others out riding.

Although only a temporary sojourner, I could not forget Creole, another mare full of quality and devilment. She came to me as a notorious one for bucking. The first time I got on her, I had a boy hold her head and mounted with due care on soft ground, walked her round gently, and when she seemed to have settled, moved off; but as soon as she got onto a really hard piece of ground, down went her head and she performed a succession of real bronco bucks, all four feet and nose together. I came off after the third, and she went on bucking for a few minutes more. However, I led her straight down to a really deep ploughland, and rode her for half an hour, taking good care to keep her head well up, so all was well. After that, I fixed a contrivance with a martingale to act as a bearing rein, the rings of the martingale (running) fastened to those of the bridoon, bringing the strap up between the ears, over the crest and to the dees of the saddle, or to my hand. This proved completely successful. I schooled her daily without further trouble, and eventually took her into practice polo, but she was not an absolutely reliable ride, though usually good fun; a bit too much riding Creole, too little of the game.

Horses, horses! Each one as I recall its individual characteristics, brings to mind echoes of others that became part of my string if only for a brief stay, but there must be a limit to these equine reminiscences. (In this connection, I must warn readers, should there be any! to skip this and certain other chapters to be specified, if horses are of no particular interest.) I do remember a time when there were no fewer than seventeen on the farm, but some of these were very transitory. It is curious that over and over again it so chanced that there were eight in permanent residence; curious because, as a small child, I had announced firmly that I should have eight horses when I grew up. Why I decided on that number, it is impossible to guess!

Before closing this chapter, I must just mention one who made a very definite mark, Giaour, or Jower as we preferred to spell him, had belonged to a so-called evacuee (see Chapter 25) parked in a Durban hotel, but about to move to Jo'burg. She sent her three steeds up to me for care and exercise until such time as she should be able to arrange for stabling and/or grazing for them near her lodging. By the time she sent for them, asking me to fix transport by rail,

Jower had become a more than favourite mount for Muriel Coote; she loved him and could not bear to think of losing him. As if anxious to cooperate, he went dead lame the very day before departure was fixed. I contacted the owner by telephone, told her he was unlikely to go sound on the hard going to be encountered round Jo'burg, whereas here on the farm, it might be hoped he would recover sufficiently to make a farm hack. At the same time, I asked if she would be willing to sell him, thereby saving the expense of transport, etc., possibly being unable to use him. She gave it thought, rang back and said we could keep him for £10. Great was the general rejoicing, and Muriel bought her own horse, much desired indeed.

As soon as we returned to the farm, having railed the other two, his new owner gazed rapturously on her very own Jower! He forgot his lameness very shortly, and never went lame again, even though she rode him on our 180-mile ride up into the mountains. He had been so seriously unsound at the vital time; we had no conscience about the deal at all. He was always a joy, absolutely reliable once you were used to his one little foible, a complete pirouette on the spot when excited at the start of a gallop in company.

Enough of horses as individuals, they gave me endless pleasure, and the satisfaction of riding one that I had handled myself from the very start was intense; lunged, long-reined, bridled, accustomed to my voice and certain simple, definite commands; mounting when it came to the point became no problem at all, and schooling progressed gradually, with enjoyment for both horse and rider. The fascination never palled.

My stable fitted in with sheep-farming very well. The shearing shed, which only had to assume that role in November, or, at earliest, late October, when the polo season was over, turned into an excellent stable the following winter, loose-boxes being adapted by means of sizeable poles. I made splendid horse-rugs from wool bales, or rather wool packs, these judiciously cut, turned in, lined with a kaffir blanket, and stitched with the blue twine supplied with the packs for sewing up the full bales, made quite tidy looking rugs, and very efficient, strong and warm, the open end of the pack slit half-way and doubled over, came round in most opportune manner across the chest.

CHAPTER 29

Expedition. Thatch grass. Mvenyane. Basutoland

As the farming year went on, each day brought some incident, small or large in importance, sometimes challenging, always interesting; no two days ever exactly similar, a fascinating life full of worries, but often of amusement. How could it be otherwise, living close to the land, weather, humans and animals providing daily diversions and entertainment. A final chapter or two describing some of these varied happenings may wind up this account. From forty years on, I think back and jot down the incidents which still remain in memory, alive and clear.

There was a farm sale far off at a lonely Berg farm, the owner gone to the war, the wife, unwilling to stay alone, had gone to relations, they had given up the farm. It bordered a native location and was liable to be handed over to add to the Bantustan in any case. I had bought, or rather agreed a price for, whatever that grass had been cut and left bundled, but lying out where it was cut. I sent a wagon up to collect, a long trek, involving a night on the way. I myself went up to the last white farm before native territory, borrowed a very nice polo pony from the kind farmer, and rode on up to this remote farm. It was very lovely on the upland, riding over the mountainous country of the foothills of the Drakensberg range. I found my wagon had duly arrived, but could not find a boy on the place to direct them to the various spots where the piles of bundles were to be found; the farm seemed to be derelict so few days after the sale. I reconnoitred on my steed, and spotted all I could, the wagon was soon loaded to capacity and began the trek back. I realised there would be two more loads, so planned to ride up again on the final foray, and find some native who knew the farm and could direct us to the places where thatch-grass grew; I was glad enough to repeat that heavenly ride.

Another expedition which I remember with great pleasure, was to a farm on the extreme edge of white territory, a native location of the Transkei right on its boundary. It was in the Mvenyane district, notorious for "bad" sour farms, but beautiful and picturesque. Alas! it is ever thus, the attractive well-watered wooded farms are sour, the bare, dry, unromantic ones are "good", the veld sweet, providing good grazing. However, it was a real treat to spend a day in such lovely country, especially when, as in this case, horses were found for any visitors.

I rode with my hosts to the top of their mountain, on the shoulder of which there was a wonderful expanse of natural "bush", wild, tangled primeval forest, rich evergreens, an occasional patch of orange and red, strange gaunt limbs hung with lichens, and underfoot, boulders and sudden springs, all mysterious and alluring. We dived into its deeply shadowed depths, crouching under overhanging branches, threading our way past great boulders, as we rode down a precipitous path on the far side of the mountain, to emerge into a little grove of almost unbelievable orange trees (so decorative) in those wild surroundings. Incredible that oranges would not only grow, but ripen at an altitude between 5,000 and 6,000 feet, but such was this small pocket of soil, snugly protected by mountain and forest, and open to the ripening South African sun.

One more of these recollections relates to a trip up into Basutoland, its closest frontier being near enough to warrant a day's drive; it was never easy to leave the farm for longer (our famous ride to the Berg needing endless organization, and planning, in a so-called quiet season).

It was a glorious drive, up and up through the heart of the Berg. After crossing the frontier, which is not imposing, a huddle of huts, one European dwelling and a couple of native policemen at the gate to search doubtful cars (which must be a dull job, as they are rare), we drove on into Basutoland – lovely rock formations, and wonderful light and shadow effects with the deep canyons and spurs. There was little stock and less habitation. We finally reached a place where we could look down from the mountain road and see the Orange river far below on its journey to the Orange Free State, to which it gives its name. This had been our goal, and from here we retraced the route, seeing ever changing views as we descended, cloud shadows chasing ahead, and getting broad smiles and greetings from the guardians of the frontier.

CHAPTER 30

Ducks. Piglets. Bushman paintings.

I found a note I had written in (presumably) 1938…... "we have heard no more of wars and rumours of wars, and hope the crisis is shelved again; apparently British Israelites predicted troubles beginning with the Ides of March, just the time of a flare-up in connection with Duff Cooper, they are counting themselves true prophets, I only hope not too true." But, "from troubles of the world, I turn to ducks," ours had been very tiresomely obstinate, insisting on establishing themselves in the henhouse each night, where they upset and muddied the drinking water, ate all the hens' food with gobblesome relish, and generally created disorder. For days, we removed them and planted them in their own quarters, but they firmly returned to their chosen resort whenever released; eventually, they started laying in one of the hens' nesting boxes, so we took a firm line, removing them and all their eggs to a nice new place of their own, shutting them in with no mercy. There they had to remain for three or four days, by which time, we hoped they would have accepted their new quarters, the eggs helping to anchor them; they did, and more were added duly, until setting took place in orderly fashion.

A kindly neighbour had started us off with the gift of a drake, a duck with ten ducklings, just hatched, and three unattached ducks with no impedimenta. These latter we called the maiden aunts. In due course, two of the aunts decided to go into partnership over a hatching venture: they sat solemnly side by side, closely wedged into – yes, the inevitable hens' nesting box! Strictly not for ducks, but there it was. They looked utterly absurd, and obviously felt rather fools, for when I approached, they shifted from one foot to the other very self-consciously, with great risk to their eggs, and hissed very faintly in a shy whisper (these were Muscovies, hence the goose-like hiss). Perhaps even more amusing, the extra aunt shared a nest with a hen. Having laid their eggs therein alternately over a period, they decided to sit together, an incongruous couple. We seemed to have characters among our fowls, for there was another hen who drank regularly with the farm cats from the same tin of milk at the same time, in truly matey fashion.

When the two aunts reached hatching time, alas! the total result was *one* duckling; we realised the assiduous turning of the whole vast clutch on the part of both would-be mothers had been such that all but one of their aspiring eggs had been outside sufficiently long to exclude all hope of a hatch. However, nothing daunted, the two parents waddled around, casting proud glances at their joint offspring, always placed carefully between them, even when taking to the water. Meanwhile, the mother duck who had arrived with family complete, made a brave show with all her ten ducklings on the waters of a little backwater in the stream below the cottage. She never led her brood to the forbidden hen-house, so they grew up without any thoughts in that direction. I loved having ducks about, they were good value, and by that, I do not mean the mercenary aspect.

So much for ducks, my mind turns to pigs, another facet of the vast mosaic of our varied farming pattern, albeit a small one, for we only kept a couple at a time, to make use of household scraps and provide bacon for the year. The first occupants of our so-called sty were two small black weaners, who arrived in a sack in a wheelbarrow from our neighbour on the hill. We decanted them into their new home with tempting feed, a clean bed, and all that little pigs should desire, but they nosed round until they found a just possible exit through the wire, out they got, and trekked off home up our hill camp with unerring instinct, despite the sack. They duly reached their mother, while we set to and made their fortress impregnable (from within), we hoped; then off we set to fetch them back. Thereafter peace.

On a farm not too far off for a morning's ride, there were said to be Bushman paintings, this indeed proved to be so. We found some very impressive paintings on the underside of a rock, protected from weathering by its own overhang. The drawings were far less crude than I had imagined, mostly of some kind of bushbuck, with an excellent idea of foreshortening which surprised me. The colours also were marvellous, and had lasted amazingly well; they must have been done with natural dyes mixed with animal fat, we thought.

CHAPTER 31

Riems. Native names. Christmas.

It is curious how memories come back as I write, recalling odd events and happenings in apparently random fashion, the mention of animal fat in my last sentence reminds me of a familiar task on the farm. Perhaps I might gather up a few of these odds and ends in a final chapter.

So, to return to the animal fat, I think of the making of riems, probably strange to many, including the meaning of riem. This is what is in general use on all South African farms, taking the place of a rope in every kind of circumstance. Leading a span of oxen (usually by a diminutive umfaan), a riem is tied round the horns of the lead ox and held by the said umfaan. Anything that needs to be tied up calls for a riem or riems, frequently broken machinery can be held together temporarily by the same means. African milkers invariably think it essential to tie the cow's hind legs before sitting down to the job, each one has his own riem for just that, often quite unnecessary, but they feel secure against the possible kick. The interesting part is in the making: first you need a dead beast, so when a cow or ox dies, as die they may despite all our care, the hide is immediately put to use (as indeed are all other parts, with the inevitable exception of the gall-bladder, though even that, I suppose, did its bit in the soil).

It is a long process, involving soaking the hide in a stream for several days, then cutting it in long, continuous strips, round and round, the hide being laid flat on the ground; boys were very practised in the art with their knives well sharpened for the job. The resultant pliable length is then looped loosely in several coils round a convenient stout branch of a tree, well up to weight, and through a kind of "handle" of wood wired very strongly to a vast rock. This huge weight, once made, is kept on every farm for all subsequent riem makings.

This rock is supported on a barrel under the branch, while the riems to be are looped into place, then the barrel is pushed away and the weight swings from the riems, pulling them out. A boy then puts a stick through the loops, and walks round and round until they are twisted up as tight as they will go, the weight thus being swung high up close to the branch. The stick is then pulled out and the weight unwinds them rapidly, and having reached its limit, proceeds to wind up again in the other directly by its own momentum; the boy stands by, slips his stick in again at the moment when it loses pace and is about to unwind, and finishes the winding up in that direction, the whole process being repeated ad infinitum. The first day or two, the object is to squeeze out all water; once this has been done thoroughly, mutton fat or lard is rubbed in in quantity, and the twisting process repeated for days until the fat has been squeezed well into the leather, resulting in beautiful, pliable, soft, weather-resistant riems for all purposes.

Although much of the daily work was obviously repetitive, there were unfailing moments of humour and indeed delight occurring in the midst of the most humdrum tasks; largely made delightful by the character of these simple, kindly, gay and generous Africans; however tiresome, however many headaches they gave me by the way!

I recall setting a small bunch of women to work to whitewash the walls of our cottage, and resurface the mud floors. For some reason, they all wanted to have a brush and whitewash, preferring that job to that of spreading daga (mud) evenly and smoothly on the floors. There were only two brushes anyway, so to resolve the argument, I stood them round me in a semi-circle, all grown up married women as they were, and solemnly counted round using the Templer-Prior version of "eeny, meeny, miny, mo," i.e., "Ickery, airy, oosan, ann, fillipy, fallipy, Nicholas John, cooby, corby Irish Mary, sinkum, sankum, buck, you're it." The two whose lot it was to wield the brushes seized them joyfully and began, while the others agreed happily that I had counted fairly, and went off cheerfully to fetch their daga. Shades of childhood games!

Native names, those bestowed on the whites of the neighbourhood (as touched on in Chapter 14) are amazingly revealing. Their uncanny gift for picking out an attribute, a characteristic, often one that might well be obscure, even hidden, was fascinating. Without going into those of our neighbours, our own will suffice to give an idea of this facility.

My daughter was known as "msa" or "momsa," which they interpreted as "gay," "joyous;" this in the early days when she was always dancing around, skipping about in high spirits. Later, to her chagrin, she acquired a second name, "mabutswa," meaning lazy, perhaps earned sometimes, but that was when she was considerably older; they still used that first name, for she was always full of jokes, and light-hearted questionings, and there were beams of welcome for her at all times.

James also earned more than one name as he grew. Having arrived aged three, and a fairly portly three at that, he was naturally "amafuta," "fat," a reflection on his figure, but he soon grew out of that and was called "makowlan," I can only write it phonetically; it signified "big chief," or so they told me. They said he would be their chief, and at a very early age, he was able to oversee for me in many directions on the farm, and even did a good deal of instruction of raw new house-girls, straight from their native locations, never having seen the inside of the home of an "umlungu," "whiteman." If I were out farming, he was on hand to show them how to lay the table!

My own names were firstly and inevitably linked with horses, "momahashe," "woman of the horses," but the subtle one was "nomaomba," the meaning of which I found it hard to unravel. Eventually, I discovered it bore reference to my habit of looking into corners and pointing out forgotten cobwebs, insisting on the removal of dust from all crannies. So it might be connected with attention to detail of "fuss-bags!" They seemed to take it in very good part, and tried hard to carry out my odd desires.

Sometimes, when I was keeping them up to the mark in this way, I would say, "What is that name you call me? Have you forgotten?" They would all laugh, but good-naturedly clean the more thoroughly. I now remember, for a short time, I had "nyakama" for a name when I first arrived in the country; it signified "frown," for they said I frowned in the effort to find the right word or expression in their language. As that problem eased with constant practice, the name dropped away, was forgotten, and only returns momentarily as I write. What interesting people they were, and how lucky I was to work with them.

The many odd jobs which had to be fitted in among the far more important real farm doings often involved considerable head-scratching: how bets to contrive, how to arrive at reasonable compromise, how to adapt material at hand, but the final achievement gave such satisfaction, there was ample reward. That bath described earlier, how well worth doing without for so long, for the delight when it was attained eventually. I revelled in the very thought for ages as I waited to find a suitable cheap one, priced down because of an almost invisible chip on the rim. Small things, but much joy in attainment.

Christmas was always a great occasion with the Africans on the farm. After milking and a due pause for breakfast and personal adornment, they would gather on the lawn in front of the cottage: the boys, their wives, grandmothers, aunts, umfaans, house girls, every kind of relation, who inevitably became attached to one or other of the huts, and of course, all the children; all dressed in their best, a colourful throng. I gave them all a short talk, wishing them a happy day, but urging them to turn up for milking in the evening sufficiently sober to do their jobs. Then each came up in turn and we gave out the presents. Every farm boy had a shirt and a pair of trousers, each working umfaan a shirt and sweets; each wife a dook (headscarf) and a packet of tea; the house girls a dress length and dook; and all the children scrambled for sweets. Finally we gave a sheep or two to kill and share out. When they had received their presents, they put them on the ground, danced round them, clapping and chanting.

We then repaired to our farm church, always beautifully decorated for the occasion by those living nearest to it. There were pleasant greetings outside after the service; we felt very glad again to belong to such an exceptionally nice community.

CHAPTER 32

Fishing. Library. Africaaner liaison

An interlude in the farming nose-to-the-grindstone pattern was a blissful week in the Drakensberg area with the Staffords (our first hosts in the country and indeed those who had inspired the very start of our faming venture). Colonel P.B. had suggested introducing me to the art of trout fishing, wet fly; to this end, he had taught me how to cast on his lawn. They took me up to the mountains with them and all the gear, he lent me rod, flies, landing net, basket, etc.; this with Mrs. P.B.'s painting kit was packed into the car, and we set off in holiday mood.

It was a perfect break, in the most glorious country imaginable. We stayed at a farm high up in the mountains, far away, the wonderful range of the Drakensberg towering above us. The country is wild and reminded me of Scotland, with patches of heather here and there; through it all curves and twists a lovely trout river, clear brown water broken by fine craggy rocks. Just to be in that country would be pleasure enough, but I had the added thrill from my first experience of real trout fishing. Colonel P.B. had been marvellously kind, not only fitting me out with all the paraphernalia, and making all necessary arrangements, but also giving me excellent coaching.

I had luck, and managed to catch at least three fish each day, so felt I had really begun. The three of us went out all day, taking a picnic lunch. Two of us fished all morning, one working upstream, the other down, while Mrs. P.B. painted. We foregathered for lunch and a crossword, then a laze with a book, finally more fishing till dusk. An ideally relaxing week offering much of value to body, mind and spirit. Then back to work with renewed vigour.

When I left England in 1937 for South Africa, I thought I should be so far from civilization on a remote farm that books would be practically unobtainable. Accordingly, I took out a vast packing case filled to the brim with the books I felt to be essential to life. However, our nearest little dorp, which boasted a post office, a general store, a butcher, no doctor or chemist, but a railway station (two trains a day, one up from Natal, one down thither; this latter gave a blast on its whistle as it arrived at Cedarville, which carried across the Flats which lay between the farm and the line, and was the signal by which the house girls timed their return from the kraal to our cottage to prepare supper), and surprisingly the trump! A library. The librarian, a stone deaf Dutch woman, had few ideas apart from the light literature supplied to the local community, both Dutch and English, apparently unquestioned so far. It was not long before I went on to the committee, and became the member responsible for ordering books. Fortunately, thanks to faithful packages of the review pages of the Sunday Times and the Times Literary Supplement, which arrived from England unfailingly (my sister-in-law the kind supplier), I was able to prepare lists with backing for each suggested title. No-one else seemed to have access to reviews, so my selection was almost automatically approved. I did take care to include a variety for all tastes!

Having to go in for meetings from time to time, I would try my luck at the market: some eggs, butter, a boiling fowl, cauliflower, anything that came to hand.

There was quite a large Dutch element in Cedarville, many of the farms on that side of the Flats being owned by Africaaners, whereas on our side, it so happened that the great proportion were English, South African born but with British forbears. As a rule, there was very little getting together of Dutch and British, the different backgrounds being responsible to some extent; but during the war years there were two or three occasions when special efforts were made to bring the races together amicably, to cement the relations.

One was a huge "Braaivleis," (the equivalent of a barbecue) in Cedarville, another a really inspiring church service for all denominations. Both the Dutch Reformed Church minister, and our own Church of England parson were joined by a Wesleyan minister, all sharing in the conduct of the service, which was taken partly in Dutch (or Africaans), partly in English. The Wesleyan minister was particularly impressive, speaking very well, and forcibly in fine English with an excellent delivery. I felt it a most splendid occasion, bringing the races and denominations together in a common effort towards peace in the world.

Later, there was a reception for Senator Myburgh, the President of the South African Senate. He is an East Griqualand farmer, who had been to England to represent South Africa. The neighbourhood was anxious to welcome him back and to hear of his trip. I think the gathering that evening may have done a great deal of good, as it was well attended by Dutch and British, and the senator stressed the need for forgetting our differences in the present crisis (as it was then), and getting along together. He brought a hopeful message from England, being impressed by the single-minded purpose of her peoples. The Dutch Reform Predikant was an excellent man, doing much to help towards unity, sinking petty difference in the face of world unrest. The speeches were interspersed with musical items from local worthies. Two violin solos, painfully out of tune, but one local farmer's wife sang delightfully, having a really lovely contralto voice.

CHAPTER 33

Feelings for the life

During those first war years when I was on my own, I could not complain I was lonely, for there was no time for loneliness. Apart from running the farm, there was housekeeping, cake-making, overseeing garden work, dressmaking for my schoolgirl daughter, teaching her young brother until he was old enough to go to boarding school. The evenings were very much occupied keeping up with the various accounts, herd-book, milk-records, farm diary, etc., etc. I would go over to the kraal early during milking, arrange the day's work with individual boys, settling any knotty point; later, riding round to see how the jobs were going.

At intervals one or other would come up to tell me of some unexpected event. They would bring up the heifers from the Flats, saying they were hungry, for example. I then had to decide whether they ought to start having feed, or whether it might not last out the winter if we began so soon. I probably compromised by keeping them up at the top of the farm, under my eye, but still on the veld. Then, as soon as I saw signs of falling off the least bit in condition, I could start giving them a little extra.

Or they would come to say the electric fence, "ayi vuma," which means literally, "doesn't want to!" That would involve a ride down the Flats, hoping to find some simple answer, such as long grass touching and causing a short, or terminals needing a clean; great relief when the problem was resolved.

The whole life, as I have said before, became the most satisfying and fulfilling imaginable. All the farm details were of absorbing interest to me (though perhaps they become wearisome to my readers, for which I apologise and recommend some judicious skipping, as suggested in my foreword for the unhorsey!) after all, those very details do vitally affect the farmer's living, his daily bread.

We had become thoroughly adapted to the conditions, never considering the purchase of anything without thinking how to contrive a substitute from materials on the spot; improve or do without. Many things once considered necessities, we discovered could be left out quite comfortably.

I became deeply attached to the country itself, especially in autumn, always a favourite time, with hints of the almost unbelievable colours of winter ahead, those of the veld to contrast sharply with the brilliant greens of wheat, oats, blue barley sown for winter grazing. Fresh nippy early mornings, sunny warm days, the polo season starting, the summer rush of work over, farmers could begin to do the countless odd jobs which had to be shelved during those summer months when there was always more work than could be got through in a day. The Flats, which at first had seemed dull without trees, yet had their own especial charm, chiefly of light and colour and views of the distant mountains, which latter perhaps I miss most in my exile.

Two ever-surprising happenings each season occurred only on the Flats, one being the arrival of a pair of sea eagles by the pan down there. Rare in *South* Africa, I believe, very handsome, being white with chestnut underparts and black wings, noble birds.

The other, a vast carpet of white, coming suddenly on a spring morning when the ground had had its early watering from spring rains. Mushrooms by the thousand, more than could be imagined, always taking us by surprise. We would dismount, take off our shirts and fill them with delight, riding back with the promise of wonderful suppers for days to come. It always made us think that manna in the wilderness must have looked like this bountiful spread.

CHAPTER 34

Return to England. Ponies again. Milk recorders

On my return to England after the war, I was offered almost immediately a small 11.00 h.h. pony for my friend's children, who were missing the farm life and their ponies particularly. She was a character and most rewarding. When accompanying the family on a holiday to Devon, where I was working on a dairy farm, she thought nothing of scrambling up and over a Devon bank (intended to contain her in her paddock) to the glorious freedom of the moor.

Eventually, after three days, we finally spotted a grey pony in a small group of wild ponies just under Hay Tor. Telling the children it might *not* be their pony, being too far off to be sure, I set off to climb up to the gathering. As I came near, I whistled her accustomed call, up went her head, and, miraculously, she detached herself from the charms of a weedy young entire and came to me. Delight of the children of course, but we were too far from the farm to let them ride back, so I rode her bareback all the way across the moor.

In due course, a foal appeared, and was spurned instantly; the little mare would acknowledge no offspring fathered by that weedy young stallion at Hay Tor. However, an obliging stand-in, borrowed to relieve Whisk of her riding duties when heavy in foal, not only adopted the rejected orphan, but actually produced some milk (so strong were her maternal instincts). This was enough to keep the foal happy, and I supplemented with Whisk's own milk, which she allowed me to draw off until it dried up naturally. Eventually, we made a present of the foal to a pony-hungry girl (owning a suitable paddock); she fetched it in a taxi!

In time, Whisk was outgrown, and had to go to a good home, while I sought the next size up; and so it progressed until a 15.00 h.h. thoroughbred cross set his seal on the series; taking his place in the top Pony Club event team, before his rider went off to training college.

No transaction resulted in a loss; all replacements proved more than satisfactory; thus the charm still worked after all those years, and somehow, we managed to keep a pony for as long as there was need. Tip-top had headed an unimaginably lengthy string, *how* lucky I have been. To find grazing and keep for these ponies in their turn, I was fortunate in that. I had taken on the job of Milk Recorder after the Dairy post in Devon, and many of the farmers whose Herds I tested offered me the odd bale of hay, the use of a suitable field, or even some oats: so the luck went on.

Mention of milk recording brings back amused memories of our milk recorder at Golden Fleece. He was the funniest prim little old bachelor, who had lived with a sister in Bournemouth. We had visions of lace curtains, doilies under genteel little cakes, antimacassars, and certainly Victorian furnishings. We never learnt how he had *ever* come to South Africa, or taken on that job. It seemed utterly improbable.

He came for the night once a month to do his recording (fortunately for him, he did not have to earmark the cows or calves, which was part of my job in England: quite impossible to imagine him in that role). He had several very fixed little habits, some connected with his diet. It took him a long time to recover from the horror when my small James inadvertently opened the bathroom door, which had no lock, when Mr D. was inside. Of course, he had no means of transport, one could not imagine him at the wheel of a car, still less on a horse! So he was delivered to us by the last farmer he had visited. We in our turn took him on to his next port of call. Poor little Mr D. I suppose he returned to a decorous retirement in Bournemouth in the end, where I feel he would have felt much more at home than he ever did in South Africa on a farm. After a considerable number of years working in the one area, our local group of farmers clubbed together and gave him a gold watch. This obviously gave him real pleasure, but he put it immediately into his bank, being far too apprehensive to risk having it about on his person. I do not believe he ever had the pleasure of consulting it, but I am sure he greatly enjoyed the knowledge of that possession. Perhaps it came into its own in Bournemouth.

CHAPTER 35

Enough

With age, comes a deepening and widening of experience. Heights and depths are touched, darkness and light. Nothing can remove what has been. The South African farm lives on in memories, many of them renewed by these jottings. This was an experience, a life that is mine for ever.

Thanks

Many thanks to Karen Lyonga for her careful transcription work, to Jan Wansell for her proof reading and Jane Parker for her help with the images used in this book.

Will England

November 2020

Printed in Great Britain
by Amazon